CONTEMPLATIVE PRAYER FOR CHRISTIANS WITH CHRONIC WORRY

Contemplative Prayer for Christians with Chronic Worry presents an eight-week approach for working with recurrent worry. Each chapter offers an introduction for the week, goals, techniques, and homework. Six free audio recordings are also available to download for use when practicing the guided meditations. Clinicians and their clients will find that the workbook helps them explore ways to lessen daily worries through contemplative prayer. Relying on scriptural support, the contemplative Christian tradition, and psychological science, clients will learn how to sit in silence with God, trusting in him during moments of uncertainty, worry, and anxiety.

Joshua J. Knabb, PsyD, ABPP, is interim co-director of the master's program in counseling psychology and associate professor of psychology in the School of Behavioral Sciences at California Baptist University.

Thomas V. Frederick, PhD, is chair of the behavioral sciences department, director of the master's program in counseling psychology, and associate professor of psychology in the Division of Online and Professional Studies at California Baptist University.

Contemplative Prayer for Christians with Chronic Worry
An Eight-Week Program

by
Joshua J. Knabb and
Thomas V. Frederick

Routledge
Taylor & Francis Group
NEW YORK AND LONDON

First published 2017
by Routledge
711 Third Avenue, New York, NY 10017

and by Routledge
2 Park Square, Milton Park, Abingdon, Oxon, OX14 4RN

Routledge is an imprint of the Taylor & Francis Group, an informa business

© 2017 Joshua J. Knabb and Thomas V. Frederick

The right of Joshua J. Knabb and Thomas V. Frederick to be identified as authors of this work has been asserted by them in accordance with sections 77 and 78 of the Copyright, Designs and Patents Act 1988.

All rights reserved. No part of this book may be reprinted or reproduced or utilized in any form or by any electronic, mechanical, or other means, now known or hereafter invented, including photocopying and recording, or in any information storage or retrieval system, without permission in writing from the publishers.

Scriptures taken from the Holy Bible, New International Version®, NIV®. Copyright © 1973, 1978, 1984, 2011 by Biblica, Inc.™ Used by permission of Zondervan. All rights reserved worldwide. www.zondervan.com. The "NIV" and "New International Version" are trademarks registered in the United States Patent and Trademark Office by Biblica, Inc.™

Trademark notice: Product or corporate names may be trademarks or registered trademarks, and are used only for identification and explanation without intent to infringe.

Library of Congress Cataloging in Publication Data
Names: Knabb, Joshua J., author. | Frederick, Thomas V., author.
Title: Contemplative prayer for christians with chronic worry : an eight-week program / by Joshua J. Knabb and Thomas V. Frederick.
Description: New York, NY : Routledge, 2017. | Includes bibliographical references and index.
Identifiers: LCCN 2016029004| ISBN 9781138690936 (hardback : alk. paper) | ISBN 9781138690943 (pbk. : alk. paper) | ISBN 9781315524658 (ebook)
Subjects: LCSH: Contemplation. | Anxiety—Religious aspects—Christianity. | Worry—Religious aspects—Christianity.
Classification: LCC BV5091.C7 K56 2017 | DDC 248.3—dc23
LC record available at https://lccn.loc.gov/2016029004

ISBN: 978-1-138-69093-6 (hbk)
ISBN: 978-1-138-69094-3 (pbk)
ISBN: 978-1-315-52465-8 (ebk)

Typeset in ITC Legacy Serif
by Swales & Willis Ltd, Exeter, Devon, UK

Visit the eResource: Routledge.com/9781138690943

DEDICATION

This workbook is dedicated to the authors' wives. To Josh's wife, Adrienne, who has regularly helped him to tolerate uncertainty over the years, consistently pointing him to God whenever he has lost his footing on the treacherous roads of life. To Tom's wife, Gail, a tangible source of acceptance and support when facing the ups and downs of life together.

CONTENTS

Foreword	xi
Acknowledgments	xiii

Introduction	**1**
Chronic Worry in the Twenty-First Century	1
A Psychological Understanding of Worry	2
A Christian View of Worry	2
God's Attributes: A Refresher	3
Mindfulness as an Antidote for Chronic Worry	4
Contemplative Prayer as a Christian Alternative for Chronic Worry	4
The Purpose and Structure of the Workbook	4
Hupomone: A Hopeful Endurance	5
Struggling with Chronic Worry: Perspectives from Erin, Ryan, and Lisa	6
Exercise: Goals for the Path Ahead	7
Notes	8
References	8

Week 1—The Relationship between Uncertainty and Worry	**9**
Introduction	9
Intolerance of Uncertainty	9
Exercise: Identifying Your Beliefs about Uncertainty	10
Exercise: Identifying Your Response to Uncertainty	12
Exercise: Reflecting on Uncertainty	12
The Relationship between Intolerance of Uncertainty, Worry, and Anxiety	13
Exercise: The Worry Log	13
Positive Views of Worry that May Be Keeping You Stuck	15
Exercise: Identifying the Perceived Benefits of Your Worry	15
An Integrative Model for Understanding Christian Worry	16
Contemplative Prayer as a Strategy to Relate Differently to Uncertainty and Worry	17
Major Goals for the Eight-Week Program	19
An Overview of the Eight-Week Program	19
Preparing for the Road Ahead: Practical Considerations	20
Overcoming Challenges	20
The Serenity Prayer: Balancing Acceptance and Change by Turning to God	21
Exercise: Writing Your Own Serenity Prayer to God	21
Conclusion	22
References	22

vii

Week 2—An Introduction to Contemplative Practice   23

Introduction	23
A Brief History of Contemplative Christianity: Eastern and Western Influences	23
Wordless Prayer and the *Apophatic* Tradition	24
The Cloud of Unknowing	26
Divine Union and *Theosis*: Deepening Your Intimacy with God	27
An Integrative Understanding: The Central Ingredients of Contemplative Prayer	29
Forms of Contemplative Prayer in this Workbook	29
Letting Go of Uncertainty and Worry: Contemplation and Yielding to God's Providence	30
Contemplative Prayer in Daily Life	30
Exercise: 20 Minutes of Contemplative Prayer	31
Exercise: Recording Your Daily Efforts	32
Exercise: Journaling about Your Experience	33
Exercise: Homework for the Week	36
Struggling with Contemplative Prayer: Perspectives from Erin, Ryan, and Lisa	36
Conclusion	37
Notes	37
References	37

Week 3—Ignatian Prayer   39

Introduction	39
Characteristics of Ignatian Spirituality	39
"Prayer of the Senses"	40
Exercise: 20-Minute "Prayer of the Senses" Meditation	41
Exercise: Recording Your Daily Efforts for the "Prayer of the Senses"	43
Exercise: Journaling about Your Experience of the "Prayer of the Senses"	44
The Daily Examen	47
Exercise: Recognizing God's Presence with the Daily Examen	48
Trustful Surrender to Divine Providence	49
Exercise: "Conformity to Divine Providence"	49
Exercise: Homework for the Week	50
Finding God in the Midst of Uncertainty: Perspectives from Erin, Ryan, and Lisa	51
Conclusion	52
Note	53
References	53

Week 4—The Jesus Prayer   54

Introduction	54
A Brief History of the Jesus Prayer	54
Eastern Orthodox Spirituality and the Jesus Prayer	55
The Main Ingredients of the Jesus Prayer	56
Exercise: Reflecting on the Jesus Prayer	57
Possible Benefits of the Jesus Prayer: A Holistic Understanding	57
Exercise: Identifying Your Own Perceived Benefits of the Jesus Prayer	58
Instructions for the Jesus Prayer	59
The Jesus Prayer, Stillness, and Uncertainty, Worry, and Anxiety	60
Exercise: 20-Minute Jesus Prayer Meditation	60
Exercise: Recording Your Daily Efforts for the Jesus Prayer	62
Exercise: Journaling about Your Experience of the Jesus Prayer	63
Additional Reflections on Mercy	65

Exercise: Homework for the Week   66
Asking Jesus for Compassion and Mercy: Perspectives from Erin, Ryan, and Lisa   67
Conclusion   68
References   69

Week 5—An Introduction to Centering Prayer   **70**

Introduction   70
A Short History of Centering Prayer   71
The Main Tenets of Centering Prayer   71
Centering Prayer and the False Self   72
Centering Prayer and Silence   75
Centering Prayer and Rest   75
Centering Prayer, Surrender, and *Kenosis*   76
Centering Prayer and Receptivity   77
Centering Prayer and the *Apophatic* Tradition   78
Centering Prayer and Common Distracting Thoughts   78
Benefits of Centering Prayer: A Psychospiritual Viewpoint   79
Exercise: What Are Your Own Expectations about Centering Prayer?   80
Instructions for Centering Prayer   81
Exercise: 20-Minute Centering Prayer Meditation   81
Exercise: Recording Your Daily Efforts for Centering Prayer   82
Exercise: Journaling about Your Experience of Centering Prayer   83
Exercise: Homework for the Week   85
Resting in God's Presence: Reflections from Erin, Ryan, and Lisa   85
Conclusion   86
Note   86
References   86

Week 6—A Continuation of Centering Prayer   **87**

Introduction   87
Centering Prayer and Consenting to God   88
Centering Prayer and Openness   89
Centering Prayer and the Simple Life   89
Centering Prayer and a Gentler Approach to Life   90
Centering Prayer and Relinquishing Your Grip   91
Centering Prayer and Rest   91
Centering Prayer and the Ability to Just "Be"   92
Centering Prayer and God's Loving Arms   94
Centering Prayer and "Detachment"   94
Centering Prayer, the Contemplative Attitudes, and Jesus   95
Instructions for Centering Prayer: A Review   96
Exercise: Continuing with the 20-Minute Centering Prayer Meditation   96
Exercise: Continuing to Record Your Daily
    Efforts for Centering Prayer   97
Exercise: Continuing to Journal about Your
    Experience of Centering Prayer   98
Exercise: Homework for the Week   100
Conclusion   101
Note   101
References   101

Week 7—An Introduction to the Welcoming Prayer — 102

Introduction — 102
A Brief Overview of the Welcoming Prayer — 103
The Main Ingredients of the Welcoming Prayer — 105
Facing Uncertainty and Yielding to God's Presence:
A Two-Pronged Strategy for Worry — 106
The Story of Mary and Martha and "Being" and "Doing" — 107
Immanuel: "God Is with Us" — 108
Instructions for the Welcoming Prayer — 109
Exercise: The 20-Minute Welcoming Prayer Meditation — 109
Exercise: Recording Your Daily Efforts for the Welcoming Prayer — 110
Exercise: Journaling about Your Experience of the Welcoming Prayer — 111
Exercise: Homework for the Week — 114
Welcoming Jesus into Uncertainty and Doubt:
The Experience of Erin, Ryan, and Lisa — 114
Conclusion — 115
Notes — 115
References — 116

Week 8—Surrendering to Divine Providence in Daily Living — 117

Introduction — 117
A Review of Surrendering to God's Providence — 117
Contemplation as a Vehicle for Surrendering — 118
The Benefits of Surrender in Daily Life — 118
Looking Forward: Surrender as a Lifelong Pursuit — 119
"It Is Well with My Soul": The Hymn that Captures Surrendering to God's Providence — 120
Breathing with Christ: Cultivating an Attitude of Surrender in the Real World — 121
Exercise: Three-Minute Breathing with Jesus — 122
Surrendering in the Bible: Key Verses to Reflect on During the Day — 123
Concluding the Program with Erin, Ryan, and Lisa — 124
Conclusion — 124
Notes — 125
References — 125

Index — 126

FOREWORD

Chronic Worry: An Eight-Week Christian Contemplative Prayer Program

Mindfulness and acceptance-based approaches to cognitive behavior therapy (CBT), such as dialectical behavior therapy (DBT), mindfulness-based cognitive therapy (MBCT), and acceptance and commitment therapy (ACT), have now achieved a central place in contemporary CBT. Their major emphasis is on mindfulness—focusing attention on one's immediate experience in the present moment, with acceptance or an open, receptive, and curious mindset, and without judgment or censure. Christian approaches to ACT in particular have recently emerged, and Joshua Knabb is a leading and articulate voice in this development, having written two excellent books: *Faith-Based ACT for Christian Clients* (Knabb, 2016b) and a faith-based workbook on ACT for Christian clients (Knabb, 2016a). Now, he has co-authored with Thomas Frederick another excellent and clearly written book on an eight-week contemplative prayer program for Christians with chronic worry. This work is based on preliminary empirical research, with encouraging results that support the effectiveness of the program (Knabb et al., 2016).

This eight-week program goes beyond mindfulness to a specifically Christian approach using contemplative prayer to help Christians with the problem of chronic worry. Such worry is associated with a basic inability or struggle to accept or tolerate life's inevitable ambiguities and uncertainties, especially about the future. Knabb and Frederick describe a spiritual or Christian antidote for chronic worry that focuses on developing the following fundamental and deep beliefs about God: (a) his infinite knowledge and wisdom; (b) his infinite love and goodness; and (c) his infinite presence and power. They therefore state: "By learning to sit with God in silence, letting go of your own efforts to control and predict your future, we believe you will be moving in the direction of accepting the uncertainties of life—in other words, learning to surrender to God's good and active presence in your life. Through acceptance, you may find that you are no longer exhausted with the struggle, repeatedly trying to grasp at a certain future that does not exist" (p. 5).

This book contains much deep wisdom drawn from scripture and the practices of the early desert Christians and others through the centuries of church history, emphasizing the central role of contemplative prayer in overcoming anxiety and chronic worry. It includes very helpful exercises that do require some time (at least 20 minutes) each day for practicing them and benefiting from them. Examples of contemplative prayer covered include: the serenity prayer, Ignatian contemplation, the Jesus Prayer, centering prayer, and the welcoming prayer. They all help us to let go and rest in God and his loving and active presence in our lives.

Knabb and Frederick have written a book that makes a significant contribution to a distinctively Christian approach to mindfulness and beyond that focuses on contemplative prayer with all of its richness in Christian tradition and practice, grounded in scripture. It is also an excellent "self-help" book that will be of tremendous help to Christians struggling with chronic worry. It points them away paradoxically from self-help or trying so hard to help themselves, towards letting go and resting in God and trusting him because of his infinite knowledge and wisdom, love and goodness, and presence and power through Jesus Christ. May you be deeply blessed with the peace of God that transcends all understanding (see Philippians 4:6–7) as you read this book and practice contemplative prayer!

Siang-Yang Tan, PhD
Professor of Psychology
Graduate School of Psychology
Fuller Theological Seminary
Pasadena, California
and author of
Counseling and Psychotherapy:
A Christian Perspective

REFERENCES

Knabb, J. (2016a). *Acceptance and Commitment Therapy for Christian Clients: A Faith-Based Workbook.* New York: Routledge.

Knabb, J. (2016b). *Faith-Based ACT for Christian Clients: An Integrative Treatment Approach.* New York: Routledge.

Knabb, J., Frederick, T., & Cumming, G. (2016). Surrendering to God's Providence: A Three-Part Study on Providence-Focused Therapy for Recurrent Worry (PFT-RW). *Psychology of Religion and Spirituality.* Advanced online publication.

ACKNOWLEDGMENTS

A variety of individuals have helped me with this writing project. To begin, thanks to my family, including my wife, daughter, and son, who have supported me and inspired me over the years, helping me to recognize the importance of attunement in the present moment. Moreover, thanks to the reviewers, including Brad Johnson, Mark McMinn, and an anonymous reviewer, who offered valuable, detailed feedback on the proposal for this book. In addition, thanks to Anna Moore at Routledge for supporting this project, as well as George Cumming III at the Grove Counseling Center for several thoughtful comments on the eight-week program. Of course, I want to especially give thanks to God for his perfect, trustworthy attributes, which make surrendering possible. Finally, I would like to thank the reader of this book: "May the God of hope fill you with all joy and peace as you trust in him, so that you may overflow with hope by the power of the Holy Spirit."

J.J.K.

It is hard to imagine a work like this coming to completion, as so many individuals have been instrumental in it. First, my family—my wife, son, and daughter—have taught me much about being present as necessary for recognizing God's graces in relationships. Second, Dr. Dirk Davis, Associate Vice President for Academics, and all of my colleagues at California Baptist University provide a rigorous and supportive academic environment that encourages collaborative projects like this. Last, and certainly not least, learning to surrender to God has provided a new awareness and openness to my present experiences, allowing me to see God at work in the everyday. May you learn to recognize God's care for you as you learn to surrender by practicing the exercises in this book.

T.V.F.

INTRODUCTION

CHRONIC WORRY IN THE TWENTY-FIRST CENTURY

For many adults in contemporary Western society, worry is a daily experience (Tallis et al., 1994). In fact, when worry becomes unmanageable, and is combined with a variety of other symptoms, it can lead to a diagnosis of generalized anxiety disorder (GAD; American Psychiatric Association [APA], 2013). To receive a diagnosis of GAD, you need to experience worry and anxiety most of the time for at least a half-year, struggling to handle your worrying thoughts. With GAD, you must also suffer from several other symptoms, such as exhaustion, uneasiness, trouble focusing, irritation, tension, and trouble sleeping (American Psychiatric Association [APA], 2013).

If you find that you tend to worry every day, and have a difficult time functioning because of your worry, this workbook may be able to help you in your current struggles. Looking out into the future, you might anticipate that something will go terribly wrong, concluding that life will fall apart today, tomorrow, or the next day. As you become more and more preoccupied about the future, "filling in the blanks," you may become increasingly distracted. You may even struggle to put one foot in front of the other, unable to be present in the moment. When this happens, life may become unmanageable, given you are "certain" gloom awaits you just around the corner.

As a Christian, you might also find that your relationship with God has suffered along the way, struggling to trust in him as you make predictions that your life will unravel tomorrow or the next day. Rather than resting in his loving arms, you may anticipate that he will not be there for you when the storms of life inevitably come crashing down, anxiously anticipating the rain, thunder, and lightning that are slowly moving in. Feeling like one of the disciples in the boat with Jesus crossing the stormy sea (Luke 8:22–25), you may cry out to God for help–"Save me from this storm!" Unfortunately, these enduring struggles can lead to both psychological and spiritual impairment, resulting in an inability to be fully present in your most salient relationships, work life, and church activities.

Drawing from the latest research in the clinical psychology literature (Dugas & Robichaud, 2007), we will be exploring alternative ways for you to relate to your worry, helping you let go of the tendency to use worry to predict and control the future and attain certainty in an unpredictable world. Given that securing certainty outside of your relationship with God is not possible, we believe that learning to accept the uncertainty of life is a useful alternative approach to navigating through daily living. Therefore, we will be presenting one of the newest theories on worry, helping you reduce the tendency to futilely pursue a certain, predictable life.

Beyond helping you improve your psychological functioning, we believe there is a key spiritual component to your current struggles as well. In fact, from our perspective, approaching your struggle with uncertainty from a spiritual perspective is one of the best ways to address worry. As a result, drawing from both scripture and the contemplative Christian tradition, we will be working with you to learn to "rest in God," a phrase coined by Gregory the Great, sitting in silence with him in order to cultivate a deeper trust in his infinite: (a) knowledge and wisdom; (b) love and goodness; and (c) presence and power. Learning to trust in these attributes of God—he is all-knowing, all-loving, and all-powerful—on a deeper level can be especially important in your journey, since finding rest in him is possible when you have a deeper awareness of this combination of his characteristics, rooted in both scripture and your personal relationship with him.

A Psychological Understanding of Worry

If you are generally struggling with anxiety, worrying is not isolated to one particular topic. Instead, anticipating future catastrophe can occur in the context of a wide variety of life domains. As an example, you may begin to worry about paying your bills on time, expecting that you will get your electricity turned off because your check will be a day late. In turn, you might predict that you will lose your job, given the industry you are in is not financially stable. Finally, you may expect that your spouse will leave you, especially since you have not been very loving or thoughtful in recent months. Each of these thoughts, of course, is in your head, based on predictions you may have made about what *might* occur in the days, weeks, or months ahead.

Notice that the central theme of these worries is an unknown future, with worry often providing you with a range of worst-case scenarios. When uncertainty is experienced, you may begin to generate a range of outcomes, writing the tragic, concluding episode of a yet-to-be-determined finale for the miniseries of your life. Thus, a foundational ingredient of worry and anxiety is the struggle to accept life's uncertainties and ambiguities (Dugas & Robichaud, 2007). In this workbook, beginning with the first week, we will assist you in exploring how you relate to uncertainty, helping you move in the direction of accepting uncertainty, rather than futilely trying to obtain a certain future (which is not possible).

A Christian View of Worry

In addition to offering a psychological interpretation of worry and anxiety, we will be presenting a biblical viewpoint, drawing from scripture and the contemplative Christian tradition, which dates back to the experiences of the early desert Christians in Egypt, Palestine, and Syria around the third century. Within the contemplative Christian tradition, surrendering to God is a central aim, with devoted followers of Jesus balancing walking behind him and resting at his feet in order to listen to him along the way.

In our view, a spiritual understanding of the antidote for worry involves cultivating a set of deeply held beliefs about God that includes his infinite: (a) knowledge and wisdom; (b) love and goodness; and (c) presence and power. By learning to sit with God in silence, letting go of your own efforts to control and predict your future, we believe you will be moving in the direction of accepting the uncertainties of life—in other words, learning to surrender to God's good and active presence in your life. Through acceptance, you may find that you are no longer exhausted with the struggle, repeatedly trying to grasp at a certain future that does not exist.

Instead of employing worry to predict and control your future—on your own and in isolation—resting in God's arms may help you recognize that he is all you need, "transferring the reins" to him

INTRODUCTION

during instances of uncertainty, doubt, worry, and anxiety. From our perspective, this intentional pivot is reminiscent of: (a) a child running into her father's arms when she hears thunder outside her bedroom window on a cold, wet winter night; and (b) a husband trusting his wife's unwavering words—"everything will be okay because we are in this together"—after losing his job, unsure of the next steps he will need to take.

GOD'S ATTRIBUTES: A REFRESHER

Within the pages of the Bible, God's attributes and characteristics—including his infinite: (a) knowledge and wisdom; (b) love and goodness; and (c) presence and power (Grudem, 1999)—are presented in a rather coherent, consistent manner. Although it is beyond the scope of this workbook to explore *all* of God's attributes, we would like to present several that we believe are important when discussing uncertainty, doubt, worry, and anxiety in the Christian life. To be sure, from a Christian perspective, we argue that having a deeper confidence in these qualities of God—which are immutable and do not change—can help you in your daily life, reflected in the interventions we present in this workbook.

To begin, the Bible reveals that God is infinitely knowledgeable and wise—that is, he is all-knowing and omniscient—as revealed in Psalm 147:5: "Great is our Lord and mighty in power; his understanding has no limit." Moreover, God is infinitely loving and good, also referred to as omnibenevolence, as Jesus famously stated: "No one is good—except God alone" (Mark 10:18). Finally, God is active, present, and sovereign, also referred to as omnipresence and omnipotence. For example, Psalm 135:5–7 declares: "I know that the Lord is great, that our Lord is greater than all gods. The Lord does whatever pleases him, in the heavens and on the earth, in the seas and all their depths. He makes clouds rise from the ends of the earth; he sends lightning with the rain and brings out the wind from his storehouses." In fact, Psalm 139:1–18 seems to especially capture God's attributes:

> You have searched me, Lord, and you know me. You know when I sit and when I rise; you perceive my thoughts from afar. You discern my going out and my lying down; you are familiar with all my ways. Before a word is on my tongue you, Lord, know it completely. You hem me in behind and before, and you lay your hand upon me. Such knowledge is too wonderful for me, too lofty for me to attain. Where can I go from your Spirit? Where can I flee from your presence? If I go up to the heavens, you are there; if I make my bed in the depths, you are there. If I rise on the wings of the dawn, if I settle on the far side of the sea, even there your hand will guide me, your right hand will hold me fast. If I say, "Surely the darkness will hide me and the light become night around me," even the darkness will not be dark to you; the night will shine like the day, for darkness is as light to you. For you created my inmost being; you knit me together in my mother's womb. I praise you because I am fearfully and wonderfully made; your works are wonderful, I know that full well. My frame was not hidden from you when I was made in the secret place, when I was woven together in the depths of the earth. Your eyes saw my unformed body; all the days ordained for me were written in your book before one of them came to be. How precious to me are your thoughts, God! How vast is the sum of them! Were I to count them, they would outnumber the grains of sand—when I awake, I am still with you.

As this powerful passage from David reveals, God truly knows you, given he is all-knowing. Also, he is everywhere, active and present in your day-to-day functioning. Therefore, God is always with you, moving within your inner *and* outer world, even when you feel alone and uncertain about what lies ahead. Further, God cares for you and has your best interests at heart—despite the storms of life. In fact, because God is all-knowing, all-loving, and all-powerful, he is an especially important ally in your struggles with uncertainty, doubt, worry, and anxiety.

Mindfulness as an Antidote for Chronic Worry

In the last decade, mindfulness meditation has been explored frequently in the clinical psychology literature as an intervention for recurrent worry (Delgado et al., 2010; Orsillo & Roemer, 2011). With mindfulness, you are focusing on one thing at a time, rooted in the present moment. When you notice your mind has been distracted by a thought or feeling, your job is to non-judgmentally and compassionately acknowledge the inner event that has pulled you away, before returning to the predetermined point of concentration.

When applying mindfulness to chronic worry, the most salient benefits include focusing on the present moment (as opposed to a catastrophic prediction about the future) and relating to thoughts and feelings with compassion and non-judgment (rather than assuming your worrying thoughts are "true" and your anxiety-related feelings need to go away).

Originally developed within the Buddhist tradition, mindfulness has more recently been "secularized" in clinical psychology, meaning it has been used as a coping skill for chronic worry, rather than embraced as a religious worldview. Yet, as a Christian, you may be wondering whether or not the Christian tradition has its own meditative heritage to draw from. In our view, Christian contemplative practices provide some of the same pragmatic, practical benefits as mindfulness for relating differently to worry and anxiety, with the added benefit of moving you in the direction of deepening your relationship with God.

Contemplative Prayer as a Christian Alternative for Chronic Worry

With contemplative prayer, you are learning to sit in silence with God, typically focusing on the breath or a prayer word to deepen your awareness of his active, loving presence (Frenette, 2012). When you are distracted with a thought or feeling, you simply acknowledge the experience, before gently returning your focus to the breath or a prayer word. Rather than the word serving as some sort of mantra to achieve an enlightened state, the word represents your willingness to focus on God, letting go of your own efforts to understand him through the mediums of cognition and affect. Over time, you are learning to rest in his presence, spending roughly 20 minutes per session in silence with him. Eventually, you may begin to find comfort in this time, letting go of the tendency to chase or push away distressing thoughts, feelings, and sensations, especially the uncertainty, doubt, worry, and anxiety you may be experiencing.

Given some of these benefits, we believe that contemplative prayer can help you relate differently to these distressing inner experiences, learning to sit at Jesus' feet (see Luke 10:38–42) as you focus exclusively on him. In this eight-week program, you will be trying on several contemplative forms of prayer in order to surrender to God, trusting in his wisdom and knowledge, loving goodness, and presence and power. Combined, these attributes can help you relinquish your own efforts to attain certainty, falling into God's proverbial arms as you spend time with him.

The Purpose and Structure of the Workbook[1,2]

The purpose of this eight-week program is to help you relate differently to your chronic worry, given that we believe a central component of your worry is the inability to tolerate uncertainty; that is, your struggles may emanate from an attempt to gain certainty about the domains of experience that are outside of your control. Grounded in the clinical psychology literature, intolerance of uncertainty (IU; Dugas & Robichaud, 2007) will be explored in the next chapter. As a fitting alternative to mindfulness meditation, we argue that contemplative prayer can help you accomplish two important tasks in your efforts to relate differently to worry.

First, daily contemplative prayer can assist you in letting go of your own efforts to attain certainty, which can make your worry and anxiety worse. Second, and equally important, contemplative prayer is about finding rest, learning to trust in God, acknowledging (and surrendering to) God's active presence. Therefore, we believe that this approach can help you improve both your psychological and spiritual functioning as you gain a greater awareness of God's active, loving presence from moment to moment.

To use this workbook, our hope is that you are already working with a mental health professional in a professional counseling or psychotherapy environment, with your counselor or therapist assisting you as you move through each week. Moreover, you may already have been diagnosed with GAD, as described earlier in this introduction. Or, you may not meet the full criteria for a formal diagnosis; instead, you might simply be struggling with daily worry, which you find is negatively impacting one or more areas of your life. In either case, this workbook will be most helpful for Christian clients who are devoted to the Christian faith and looking to relate differently to uncertainty, doubt, worry, and anxiety because your previous efforts have not succeeded.

Instead of trying to control your worry and anxiety, accepting these symptoms and relating differently to them by yielding to God's providential care may be the solution you are looking for. In the first week of the program, you will learn more about the role that IU (Dugas & Robichaud, 2007) plays in maintaining your struggle with worry and anxiety. After the first week, you will begin to practice several contemplative exercises to help you let go of your own efforts to attain certainty and control. You will be working on cultivating a deeper trust in God's protective care by spending time with him in silence. In these remaining weeks, you will learn several contemplative forms of prayer, practicing connecting to God in each moment, especially when you feel uncertain and anxious about what lies ahead.

Hupomone: A Hopeful Endurance

Within this eight-week program, you may find the daily practices to be especially challenging, given we are asking you to sit in silence with God for extended periods of time. Further, this sitting in silence seems counterproductive—you are not actively engaging in actions to attain certainty, which seems like a logical solution. Still, since many of your prior efforts have led to added frustration and pain, we ask that you press forward, trusting God in the process to plant seeds that may sprout at a later time. In other words, rather than expecting immediate results, including a "feeling" of elation or happiness, our hope is that you will remain patient, balancing connecting to God in the present moment with looking ahead to a future filled with a deeper union with him.

Within the New Testament, the Greek word *hupomone* seems to best capture this attitude we are referring to. Meaning a hopeful, constant endurance (Strong, 2001), *hupomone* is often translated as "patience" in the New Testament. Yet, beyond patience, *hupomone* has an extra element of hope, denoting the ability to endure both inner and outer trials because of Christians' hope in Jesus' redeeming, sacrificial act upon the cross (Ephesians 1:7) and his eventual restoration of this broken world (Revelation 21).

Overall, as you move through the program, our hope is that you will continue to walk towards God, even when your uncertainty, doubt, worry, and anxiety seem to be especially distressing. Along the way, you may find that your time spent with him is even more important than the elimination of your pain. After all, the *complete* eradication of worry and anxiety is not likely to happen during your God-given time on this planet.

Before beginning the eight-week program, we would like to introduce you to three individuals who will be walking with you along the way. Each of these adults struggles with recurrent uncertainty, worry, and anxiety, which manifests in their life in unique ways. Still, as you travel with them, our hope is that they can help you better understand the material, including how to "try on" the exercises and "stay the course," pressing forward even when your mind tells you to turn around and head back home.

STRUGGLING WITH CHRONIC WORRY: PERSPECTIVES FROM ERIN, RYAN, AND LISA

For Erin, uncertainty was always difficult to tolerate. At the age of seven, her parents divorced, which came as a sudden shock. When her parents broke the news, she felt extremely anxious about what might happen next, frequently worrying that her parents did not love her anymore. In fact, Erin continuously struggled with anticipating a worst-case scenario, which involved her father moving out of the home and never returning.

Over time, Erin began to expect that the worst would happen in almost all areas of life. If she anticipated even a little uncertainty about her future, her mind would quickly generate a long list of doomsday predictions. From Erin's perspective, preparing herself for a wide variety of negative outcomes protected her from a sudden shock, something she vowed she would never experience again after her parents broke the unexpected news of their severed relationship.

In fact, prior to her parents' divorce, Erin felt a tremendous sense of safety, recalling how excited she would get about going to Sunday School at her local church, learning about Jesus' loving presence. She was especially drawn to images of Jesus with small children, protecting them from harm as they sat at his feet. Yet, after the divorce, she struggled to view God as a loving, protecting father; instead, she would frequently try to attain her own certainty, managing whatever she could control in her environment. Over time, her autonomy developed into a pattern that extended to all areas of life, including her intimate relationships, work life, and experience of God.

With Ryan, life seemed to be relatively stable and predictable until he went to college. In his freshman year, he began to date a woman whom he was convinced he would eventually marry. From his perspective, she was beautiful, loving, and smart, important qualities that he saw in his mother growing up. To be sure, in his childhood, Ryan observed his parents as loving, nurturing, and supportive, leading to a view that life was going to be all right.

Growing up in the church, Ryan learned about God's wisdom, goodness, and power, seeing God as active in his daily life as he transitioned into adulthood. In fact, Ryan frequently remembered praying to God for protection, trusting that God would provide for him in each passing moment. As he went off to college, he was hopeful that God would continue to meet his needs.

After a few years of dating, Ryan began to notice that his girlfriend was pulling away. Anticipating that he was losing her, he tried repeatedly to talk to her about his observations. However, she seemed to be unresponsive, failing to return his calls or show up for dates. Eventually, she had the "dreaded" conversation with him, letting him know she was dating someone else.

When Ryan received this news, he was absolutely crushed, struggling to make sense of how God could allow this to happen. After all, he was convinced that God had strategically placed this woman in his life, and could not understand why God would unilaterally take her away. In his senior year of college, Ryan began to struggle with generalized anxiety, doubting that God would provide and striving to attain certainty in order to protect himself from another sudden

INTRODUCTION

surprise. As a result, he found himself procrastinating about making decisions, isolating himself whenever he felt uncertain about a dating relationship.

Lisa always described herself as a worrier, growing up in a home without a mother. In her childhood, her father needed to provide for the family, resulting in him coming home late most nights. Lisa was frequently alone as a child, worrying about everything from "robbers breaking into the house" to not having help with her homework. In her middle childhood years, she developed generalized anxiety, struggling to accept the uncertainty of life. In Lisa's world, uncertainty was especially dangerous, given that she did not have anyone to tell her things would work out in life.

Yet, as a young adult, she met her husband, a supportive, warm, and caring man, and settled down to start a family. After raising two children, she eagerly anticipated the time she could finally spend with her husband, given the kids were off to college. On one summer evening, she received a phone call from the police department, with a stranger on the other end of the line telling her that her husband had just died in a car accident on a local freeway.

Absolutely devastated, she did not know what to do. In her adult years, she had learned to trust in both her husband and God, given that she finally had a support system that helped her to endure the pains of this world. In church life, she was learning to radically trust in God, recognizing that he had a special plan for her. In the months following her husband's death, though, her generalized anxiety from childhood quickly returned.

As Lisa moved through the grieving process, she felt increasingly anxious, worrying about what else might be taken from her unexpectedly. At night, while in bed, she would frequently yell at God, asking question after question about how he could let this happen. To try to obtain certainty, she found herself increasingly asking for reassurance from her adult children, preoccupied with their safety in that they lived in a distant state, away at college. Moreover, she constantly searched the Internet for answers to a wide variety of problems, spending nights on end creating a pseudo-sense of certainty for an unknown future.

For Erin, Ryan, and Lisa, generalized anxiety is linked to a struggle to accept the uncertainties of life, given the traumatic events that surprised them in daily living. As a result, worry is a way to generate a false sense of certainty, using a wide variety of strategies to "fill in the blanks" of life. As you move through this program, you will continue to get to know these individuals, beginning in the second week. Our hope is that you can identify with them in some way, shape, or form, given that their struggles are quite common in contemporary Western society.

EXERCISE: GOALS FOR THE PATH AHEAD

Before starting the eight-week program, see if you can jot down at least three goals, focusing on what you want to get out of this time spent with God. Try to envision "crossing the finish line" of this workbook. As you finish the race, what do you want to accomplish? How would you like to relate differently to your symptoms? How would you like to relate to God?

1. _____

_____

2. _____

_____

3. _____

_____

Notes

1 Given the application of MBCT (Segal et al., 2012) to both depressive and anxiety disorders (see, e.g., Evans et al., 2008; Teasdale et al., 2000), we have designed our eight-week program as a culturally sensitive alternative for Christian clients. Specifically, we use a Christian worldview and contemplative prayer in place of secular, mindfulness-based practices. See Knabb et al. (2016) for the original three-part study, which we also describe in more detail in a subsequent chapter of this workbook. Overall, we have converted the manualized treatment approach from Knabb et al. into a user-friendly client workbook, significantly expanding upon the manual from the pilot study to offer a range of concepts, exercises, and practices for Christians with recurrent worry.

2 It is worth mentioning that variations of some of the integrative efforts, principles, and exercises in this workbook for Christians with chronic worry are also mentioned in Knabb (2016) and Knabb (2017), with the former written as a guide for clinicians working with Christian clients with depressive and anxiety disorders (rather than more narrowly focusing on chronic worry) and the latter serving as a client workbook version of the clinicians' guide. Also worth noting, the writings of St. Claude de la Colombière (1980), Dugas and Roubichaud (2007), and Segal et al. (2012) have especially influenced the development of our integrative approach to chronic worry.

References

American Psychiatric Association (2013). *Diagnostic and Statistical Manual of Mental Disorders* (5th ed.). Washington, DC: American Psychiatric Association.

Delgado, L., Guerra, P., Perakakis, P., Vera, M., Paso, G., & Vila, J. (2010). Treating Chronic Worry: Psychological and Physiological Effects of a Training Programme Based on Mindfulness. *Behaviour Research and Therapy, 48*, 873–882.

Dugas, M., & Robichaud, M. (2007). *Cognitive-Behavioral Treatment for Generalized Anxiety Disorder: From Science to Practice.* New York: Routledge.

Evans, S., Ferrando, S., Findler, M., Stowell, C., Smart, C., & Haglin, D. (2008). Mindfulness-Based Cognitive Therapy for Generalized Anxiety Disorder. *Journal of Anxiety Disorders, 22,* 716–721.

Frenette, D. (2012). *The Path of Centering Prayer: Deepening Your Experience of God.* Boulder, CO: Sounds True, Inc.

Grudem, W. (1999). *Bible Doctrine: Essential Teachings of the Christian Faith.* Grand Rapids, MI: Zondervan.

Knabb, J. (2016). *Faith-Based ACT for Christian Clients: An Integrative Treatment Approach.* New York: Routledge.

Knabb, J. (2017). *Acceptance and Commitment Therapy for Christian Clients: A Faith-Based Workbook.* New York: Routledge.

Knabb, J., Frederick, T., & Cumming, G. (2016). Surrendering to God's Providence: A Three-Part Study on Providence-Focused Therapy for Recurrent Worry (PFT-RW). *Psychology of Religion and Spirituality.* Advanced online publication.

Orsillo, S., & Roemer, L. (2011). *The Mindful Way Through Anxiety: Break Free from Chronic Worry and Reclaim Your Life.* New York: The Guilford Press.

Segal, Z., Williams, M., & Teasdale, J. (2012). *Mindfulness-Based Cognitive Therapy for Depression* (2nd ed.). New York: The Guilford Press.

St. Claude de la Colombière. (1980). *Trustful Surrender to Divine Providence: The Secret of Peace and Happiness.* Charlotte, NC: Tan Books.

Strong, J. (2001). *The New Strong's Expanded Dictionary of the Words in the Greek New Testament.* Nashville, TN: Thomas Nelson.

Tallis, F., Davey, G., & Capuzzo, N. (1994). The Phenomenology of Non-Pathological Worry: A Preliminary Investigation. In G. Davey & F. Tallis (Eds), *Worrying: Perspectives on Theory, Assessment, and Treatment* (pp. 61–89). Chichester, UK: John Wiley & Sons, Ltd.

Teasdale, J., Segal, Z., Williams, J., Ridgeway, V., Soulsby, J., & Lau, M. (2000). Prevention of Relapse/Recurrence in Major Depression by Mindfulness-Based Cognitive Therapy. *Journal of Consulting and Clinical Psychology, 6,* 615–623.

WEEK 1

THE RELATIONSHIP BETWEEN UNCERTAINTY AND WORRY

INTRODUCTION

In this chapter, you will learn about the role that uncertainty plays in the development and maintenance of your worry and anxiety, specifically focusing on the concept of IU. In addition, you will explore an integrative model—rooted in empirical research and the Christian faith (Knabb et al., 2016)—to help you address your recurrent worry, surrendering to God to let go of all the ways you have tried to manage your uncertainty over the years. Finally, we will introduce you to a specific type of prayer, which you will begin next week, to help you let go of your own control strategies, yielding to God's active, loving presence in the process.

Given that your responses to uncertainty and worry have probably not worked in the past, we are hopeful that you will be open to an alternative way to relate to these inner experiences, focusing on both your psychological and spiritual functioning. Before transitioning to daily contemplative practice, though, we want to provide an alternative way for you to understand: (a) your struggle with uncertainty; (b) your problematic responses to uncertainty; (c) your prior life experiences with uncertainty; and (d) the ways in which you may employ worry to increase a sense of certainty in life. To conclude this week, you will have the opportunity to write your own prayer to God, consistent with the Serenity Prayer.

INTOLERANCE OF UNCERTAINTY

According to Dugas and Robichaud (2007), experts on GAD, struggling to accept the uncertainty of life is a core feature of chronic worry. In other words, the only certainty in life is that life is uncertain. As Mathew 6:27 reminds us, "Can any one of you by worrying add a single hour to your life?" To be sure, there are several common beliefs about uncertainty that may exacerbate your worry and anxiety (adapted from Dugas & Robichaud, 2007):

- Uncertainty and ambiguity are distressing, and will get in the way of daily living.
- Uncertainty and ambiguity need to be avoided, no matter what the cost.
- Uncertainty and ambiguity are unfair, and should not be tolerated.

In terms of the first feature, you may believe that uncertainty is quite difficult to tolerate, given that even a small amount of ambiguity in life is anxiety producing for you. In fact, you may try to avoid uncertainty because of the emotional pain that you experience in uncertain situations. Over time, you might have developed the belief that, on its own, uncertainty inevitably leads to psychological turmoil.

Because of the link between uncertainty and anxiety, you might begin to avoid situations that have even the slightest degree of ambiguity, employing a wide variety of behavioral strategies to create a seemingly certain future. Yet, at a certain point, you may find that your avoidance of uncertainty is causing more problems than the actual uncertainties of life, which are inevitable and continue to arise on a daily basis. Certainly, the more you try to avoid uncertainty, the more you are faced with an increasingly uncertain future.

Finally, you might begin to believe that uncertain situations are unfair, and should not be accepted or tolerated in any way. Therefore, you may find yourself experiencing emotional distress, given your belief that normal, healthy functioning involves navigating through a certain, fixed, and predictable world. Unfortunately, when the ambiguities of life manifest, you might become easily frustrated, holding onto the notion that they simply should not exist.

With each of these beliefs, there is an underlying view that uncertainty is problematic. On the other hand, certainty, from this perspective, seems to be achievable on at least some level. As a result, your life may quickly unravel based on the reality that daily living is filled with surprises, unpredictable outcomes, and mysteries that you just cannot wrap your mind around.

Exercise: Identifying Your Beliefs about Uncertainty

In the space that follows, see if you can identify several negative beliefs you have about uncertainty. Some questions to consider:

- When you are faced with an uncertain future, what do you tell yourself?
- What are your expectations about uncertainty?
- What emotions do you feel when you are uncertain? What do you believe about this emotional experience?
- What do you do when you are uncertain? How do you make sense of this behavior?
- Do you believe you must eliminate uncertainty, no matter what the cost?
- Do you believe that uncertainty is unfair? If so, why do you believe this?
- Do you become frustrated when you are uncertain about the future? If so, why?

In addition to negative beliefs about uncertainty, we believe it is important to begin to identify your responses to the ambiguities of life. It is important to pay attention to your thoughts, feelings, and actions regarding uncertainty. As revealed by Dugas and Robichaud (2007), you may use either "approach" or "avoidance" strategies in an effort to manage uncertainty. See if you can identify some of the following strategies in your own life, which may serve the purpose of creating a seemingly certain future (adapted from Dugas & Robichaud, 2007):

- Struggling to let other people help you, given you want to make sure everything is perfect through managing tasks on your own.
- Trying to micromanage other people, given you believe that they will get hurt or make mistakes if you do not actively care for them.
- Compulsively checking tasks you have completed, fearing that you have made a mistake.
- Scanning your environment for information to make sure you have all of the "facts," whether through surfing the Internet or asking others for advice.
- Doubting your ability to problem solve, questioning whether you made the best decision after you have implemented a course of action.
- Constantly asking for support and comfort from others, often by questioning them about whether or not you made the right decision, especially when you are uncertain about the ambiguities of life.

Of course, it is helpful to ask others for feedback in a variety of situations. Here, however, we are talking about a constant "checking-in" with others in an attempt to relieve unwanted anxious feelings, not the actual "feedback" that can be helpful in collaborative situations. If you have identified with any of the above behaviors, you likely employ "approach" strategies when you are uncertain. You may try to "fill in the blanks" by pursuing certainty in an effort to attain some sort of fixed, predictable future.

On the other hand, you might find that you utilize "avoidance" strategies when you are overwhelmed with uncertainty, such as the following behaviors (adapted from Dugas & Robichaud, 2007):

- Delaying a variety of important tasks, based on the notion that you are uncertain about the outcome.
- Attempting to come up with "valid excuses" for not committing to certain behaviors, given that you are unsure about how things will turn out.
- Struggling with procrastination, "kicking the can down the road." Fearing you will make the wrong decision since you do not have all of the "facts."

With the above list, you may struggle to commit to a set of concrete behaviors, worrying that you do not have enough information to make a decision in life.

These behaviors, whether through "approaching" or "avoiding," can create added suffering for your life, since they tend to take up quite a bit of time. If you are compulsively checking by constantly reaching out to others to be soothed or comforted or searching the Internet for just the right answer, you may find you are exhausted, beyond the uncertainty and anxiety you feel in a given situation. Conversely, if you are avoiding life (based on the idea that you do not have enough information to make a decision), you might be falling behind with important tasks and suffering in your personal relationships or work life.

EXERCISE: IDENTIFYING YOUR RESPONSE TO UNCERTAINTY

In the below space, try to identify your own strategies in responding to uncertainty. Do you tend to use "approach" strategies? Or do you often avoid life when you feel you do not have enough information to make a decision? In either case, see if you can list at least five negative behaviors you engage in when you are uncertain about your future.

1. _____

_____

2. _____

_____

3. _____

_____

4. _____

_____

5. _____

_____

EXERCISE: REFLECTING ON UNCERTAINTY

Given that a possible struggle with uncertainty is a central part of your current experience, see if you can reflect on uncertainty in your life, choosing one major life experience that involved significant uncertainty and ambiguity. If you can, try to select an experience that was especially distressing, serving as a pivotal moment in your life. In other words, try to identify a foundational experience that served to solidify your belief that uncertainty is dangerous, unfair, or distressing. Some questions to consider:

- How old were you when this event occurred?
- Who was involved?
- Where were you at, in terms of the location or setting?
- What transpired, leading to significant uncertainty?
- How did you feel during this event?
- What did you do in response to your uncertainty?
- What did you conclude about uncertainty?

_____

_____

_____

_____

_____

The Relationship between Intolerance of Uncertainty, Worry, and Anxiety

In the last decade, researchers have begun to hypothesize several ways in which your struggle with uncertainty may lead to worry and anxiety (Dugas & Robichaud, 2007). To begin, you may envision a worst-case scenario unfolding because of your uncertainty, resulting in prolonged worry. Stated differently, if you do not have all of the "facts" and are missing what seems to be vital information, you may expect that a doomsday, catastrophic outcome will occur. In the process, you may struggle to embrace a "wait and see" approach. As a result, you might go over and over a range of outcomes, often the worst possible scenarios. As you continue to worry, you may find that you experience heightened anxiety.

As another possible link, you may have a tendency to require either an extensive amount of information or a long list of "facts about the case" when attempting to decide which direction to head in during instances of uncertainty. This need for additional details, even when you are facing only a benign amount of ambiguity in life, can lead to prolonged worry, ending in heightened anxiety. Stated differently, if you do not have as many details as you would like, you may employ worry as a way to predict and anticipate the future, struggling to make a decision when you are missing only a small amount of information.

As one final trajectory, you might tend to doubt your problem-solving abilities when you are facing ambiguity and uncertainty, worrying about a decision you need to make. As a result, because of your struggle to have confidence in your ability to decide the best path forward when you have missing information, you may find yourself worrying about whether or not you will succeed. In turn, you may experience elevated anxiety, given you are worrying about whether or not you will choose what is best for your life.

In each of these scenarios, uncertainty is linked to worry, with anxiety following shortly thereafter. As these situations reveal, worry is often sandwiched between uncertainty and anxiety. Therefore, beyond merely identifying your beliefs about uncertainty (and concluding that they are often negative), we believe it is important for you to identify your worrying thoughts, exploring them to see if you have certain themes that emerge in daily living.

Exercise: The Worry Log

Over the course of the next week, see if you can keep track of your worrying thoughts, which often involve predicting that something negative or catastrophic will occur in the future. As a cognitive endeavor, worrying often leads to added anxiety. Therefore, you might find it helpful to work backwards, recognizing when you are anxious. As you identify when you are feeling anxious in a given moment, see if you can pinpoint what you are thinking to yourself, including what types of predictions you are making about your future.

Day of the Week	Worrying Thoughts (Morning)	Worrying Thoughts (Midday)	Worrying Thoughts (Night)
Monday			
Tuesday			
Wednesday			
Thursday			
Friday			
Saturday			
Sunday			

After you have tracked your worrying thoughts over the course of this week, see if you can identify certain themes, including the times of day you tend to worry. What types of predictions do you make? When do you make them? Are there certain themes that emerge, in terms of the worst-case scenarios that unfold in your head? Do they involve your personal relationships, work life, church life, relationship with God, or some other area of life? See if you can write down some of the answers to the above questions, taking a step back to observe the patterns of your worry.

_____

_____

_____

_____

_____

_____

_____

_____

Positive Views of Worry that May Be Keeping You Stuck

In your current struggles with worry, you may have certain beliefs about your catastrophic predictions that are keeping you stuck. These beliefs, which can be surprisingly positive in nature, often involve the following themes (adapted from Dugas & Robichaud, 2007):

- Worrying is a great way to problem solve.
- Worrying gives me the needed motivation to accomplish a wide variety of important tasks.
- Worrying helps me to prepare myself so that I will not be surprised.
- Worrying is just part of my personality, given I am an organized, thoughtful person who takes pride in making the correct decision.

Unfortunately, these views on worry may be preventing you from letting go of your futile efforts to achieve certainty and anticipate future events. Certainly, some anxiety is helpful in life, given that it can motivate you to act, thrusting you forward to take action when you need to resolve an anticipated issue. Yet, worrying can often lead to "spinning your wheels," devoting crucial mental energy to going around in circles, not unlike being stuck on a hamster wheel.

As we will discuss in a subsequent section of this chapter, worrying can also get in the way of deepening your relationship with God, given you are focusing on *your own* efforts to predict and control the future. Yet, Jesus taught us not to worry, pointing to God's providence as a way to help Christians see that he will provide (Matthew 6:25–34). Certainly, your views on worry, in addition to the actual worry itself, may be getting in the way of your ability to let go of the grip you have on your worrying thoughts. In fact, you might be tightly clutching your worry, reminiscent of a lucky charm that you have held onto over the years, convinced that you cannot move through life without it.

Exercise: Identifying the Perceived Benefits of Your Worry

In the space that follows, see if you can identify several positive beliefs you have about your worry, focusing on the things you tell yourself so that you continue to turn to worry when you are uncertain. In other words, how have you perceived that worry has worked for you in the past?

1. _____

   _____

2. _____

   _____

3. _____

   _____

4. _____

   _____

5. _____

   _____

After this exercise, try to reflect on what themes emerged. What personal beliefs about worry are getting in the way of letting go? How, if at all, might these views serve as a barrier to ameliorating your chronic worry?

An Integrative Model for Understanding Christian Worry

In this program, you will utilize contemplative prayer as a way to let go of the tendency to pursue certainty, given that achieving certainty is impossible to do. In other words, rather than striving towards creating a permanent sense of predictability and certainty in life, you will be learning how to yield to God's protective care, reminiscent of Jesus' teaching on worry in Matthew 6:25–34. Consistent with the IU literature, struggling with accepting uncertainty often leads to recurrent worry, which exacerbates anxiety.

Within Dugas and Robichaud's (2007) cognitive behavioral manual for GAD, they advocate for accepting the uncertainties and ambiguities of life, given that the alternative—pursuing and securing a certain future—is just not possible, leading only to exhaustion and added anxiety. In other words, the best strategy for dealing with uncertainty is acceptance, rather than anxious action. As a Christian, you may also be struggling in your spiritual life based on the idea that achieving certainty on your own may be pulling you away from God. This pursuit of certainty may be undermining your ability to rest in his arms from moment to moment, trusting in him throughout your day.

Within our recent three-part study among adult Christians, we focused on a specific model of worry, hypothesizing that deeply held beliefs about God's providence (i.e., his protective, loving care) would lead to the ability to surrender to him (Knabb et al., 2016). In turn, surrendering to God would be linked to less worry, with the ability to tolerate uncertainty explaining the surrender-worry association. Among both college students and a church sample, we were able to confirm these hypotheses. In other words, as these Christians were able to view God as a provider, reminiscent of Jesus' teaching on worry in Matthew 6:25–34, they were more likely to report that they were able to surrender to him, including to his will for their life. This posture of surrendering, moreover, was associated with less worry, including the ability to tolerate the uncertainties of life.

We believe that the results of our study, noted above, are consistent with Jesus' teaching on worry within Matthew's gospel (6:25–34):

> Therefore I tell you, do not worry about your life, what you will eat or drink; or about your body, what you will wear. Is not life more than food, and the body more than clothes? Look at the birds of the air; they do not sow or reap or store away in barns, and yet your heavenly Father feeds them. Are you not much more

valuable than they? Can any one of you by worrying add a single hour to your life? And why do you worry about clothes? See how the flowers of the field grow. They do not labor or spin. Yet I tell you that not even Solomon in all his splendor was dressed like one of these. If that is how God clothes the grass of the field, which is here today and tomorrow is thrown into the fire, will he not much more clothe you—you of little faith? So do not worry, saying, "What shall we eat?" or "What shall we drink?" or "What shall we wear?" For the pagans run after all these things, and your heavenly Father knows that you need them. But seek first his kingdom and his righteousness, and all these things will be given to you as well. Therefore do not worry about tomorrow, for tomorrow will worry about itself. Each day has enough trouble of its own.

As mentioned in Jesus' famous teaching, Christians can let go of worry because of God's benevolent, loving care. Therefore, surrendering to him involves trusting in his infinite knowledge and wisdom, loving goodness, and presence and power, which we will be focusing on in this eight-week program. Certainly, Christians can let go of their pursuit of certainty, worrying to "fill in the blanks," because God is active and present from moment to moment with Christians' best intentions in mind.

In addition to exploring our model of worry, we tested this eight-week program among a sample of 13 Christians with chronic worry, with results revealing a significant reduction in worry, IU, depression, anxiety, and stress (Knabb et al., 2016). Also, there was a significant increase in terms of positive beliefs about God's providence and the ability to surrender to his will. Therefore, based on: (a) the results of our three-part study; and (b) previously established mindfulness-based interventions for chronic worry, we believe that combining the IU literature with the contemplative Christian tradition (in place of mindfulness-based practice) can help you surrender to God during instances of uncertainty, worry, and anxiety.

Overall, in the next eight weeks, we hope to help you ameliorate Christian worry, which we define as follows:

- The unsuccessful human attempt, through cognitive efforts, to obtain certainty about an ambiguous future because of the struggle to believe in, trust, and surrender to the perfect care of an infinitely wise, loving, and powerful God.

Notice, in this definition, that we capture the human struggle with uncertainty, pointing to worry as a futile way to create a certain, predictable future through the thinking process. Yet, as this definition reveals, Christians tend to employ worry as a way to obtain certainty *on their own*, struggling to yield to *God's* omniscience, omnibenevolence, omnipresence, and omnipotence. God's attributes, from our perspective, can help you to relinquish the grip you have on worry, given that God knows the future, has your best intentions in mind, and is always present, with absolute power to orchestrate your future endeavors.

Contemplative Prayer as a Strategy to Relate Differently to Uncertainty and Worry

From our viewpoint, contemplative prayer can help you work towards surrendering to God's active, loving presence, letting go of the tendency to employ worry to predict and control your future. Because worry can be distracting, increasing your anxiety and leading to exhaustion, we are hopeful that daily contemplative practice can move you in the direction of adopting a yielding attitude, resting in God's arms because of his loving care for you. As you sit with him in silence, relinquishing your own efforts—through cognitive means—to manage both your inner and outer world, we believe you will slowly learn to relate differently to your worry and anxiety.

Essentially, we are talking about trusting in God's *providence*, or his active, loving presence in the world. Reminiscent of Matthew 6:25–34, God cares for you, actively intervening in your life with infinite knowledge and wisdom, love and goodness, and presence and power. Interestingly, Laird (2006) recently described contemplative prayer as "the practice of silence," "the silence of surrender," and "interior stillness" (p. 3), noting that the practice is about "a surrendering of deeply imbedded resistances that allows the sacred within gradually to reveal itself as a simple, fundamental act" (p. 8).

Contemplative prayer allows us to deeply experience God's active presence within our inner-most being. The result is an increased ability to surrender our futile efforts to control our lives and rely on God's grace and goodness. This type of spiritual discipline allows us to become aware of God's grace and activity both internally and externally, helping us to respond differently to our anxiety and worry. As a result, we experience freedom from the need to obtain certainty in our efforts and trust deeply in God's goodness.

For Keating (2002), contemplative prayer is defined as follows:

> The laying aside of thoughts. It is the opening of mind and heart, body and feelings—our whole being—to God, the Ultimate Mystery, beyond words, thoughts, and emotions. We do not resist them or suppress them. We accept them as they are and go beyond them, not by effort, but by letting them all go by. We open our awareness to [God] whom we know by faith is within us, closer than breathing, closer than thinking, closer than choosing—closer than consciousness itself. (p. 137)

In terms of the strengths of contemplative practice, Foster (2001) recently offered the following qualities:

- Contemplative practice can help you to deepen your love of Jesus, placing him at the center of your existence.
- Contemplative practice can help you to move beyond abstract thoughts about God, experiencing him on a much deeper level.
- Contemplative practice can help you turn to prayer as a salient vehicle through which you can relate to God.
- Contemplative practice can help you to spend more time with God in solitude, cultivating a deeper union with him by focusing on intimacy and connection.

To summarize the above definitions, qualities, and strengths of contemplative practice, this silent, wordless form of Christian prayer is about letting go of your own cognitive efforts, relinquishing the control you employ in an effort to create certainty. Instead, you are learning to sit in silence with God, resting in his arms because you trust that he is active and present within. Rather than using thoughts and feelings to relate to him, you are basking in the simplicity of a wordless, silent state, spending time with God in solitude in order to cultivate a deeper trust in his knowledge and wisdom, love and goodness, and presence and power. Over time, we believe that you will develop an attitude of trust, letting go of your need to use worry to create a pseudo-sense of certainty and security. Consistent with Jesus' teachings on worry in Matthew 6:25–34, you will be moving in the direction of focusing on God in the present moment, who sustains you and carries you along the paths of life.

Major Goals for the Eight-Week Program

In this eight-week program, our three major goals for you are as follows:

1. You will learn about a Christian model of worry that suggests Christians experience recurrent worry and doubt due to the struggle to regularly surrender to God's providential care; over time, you will learn to accept uncertainty because God is infinitely knowledgeable and wise, loving and good, and present and powerful.
2. You will learn about the contemplative Christian tradition, including a variety of daily contemplative practices to deepen your union with God, beyond thoughts, feelings, and sensations.
3. During moments of uncertainty and worry, you will learn to use a variety of contemplative strategies to "rest in God's arms," rather than using your own futile efforts to create certainty through worry and "approach" and "avoidance" strategies.

An Overview of the Eight-Week Program

Below is a basic overview of the program, which includes the concepts and practices you will learn about each week:

*   Week 1—You will learn about the relationship between uncertainty, worry, and anxiety, as well as a Christian understanding of worry. Moreover, you will begin to explore the contemplative Christian tradition to help you with your uncertainty and worry, surrendering to God, instead of trying to attain certainty through worrying efforts.
*   Week 2—You will learn more about contemplative prayer, including its history within the Christian tradition and application to uncertainty and worry. From Week 2 forward, you will be practicing daily contemplative prayer in order to yield to God's active, loving presence during instances of uncertainty, worry, doubt, and anxiety.
*   Week 3—You will learn about Ignatian contemplation, which can help you to embed yourself within a biblical story. Within this practice, you will be relating to Jesus' teaching on worry in a new way, feeling your way into this famous passage in the gospel of Matthew in order to surrender to God's providential care during moments of uncertainty and worry.
*   Week 4—You will learn about the Jesus Prayer, applying this type of contemplative prayer to your struggles with worry and anxiety. You will have the opportunity to practice the Jesus Prayer daily in order to reach out to God, asking for him to show you mercy (i.e., loving compassion) whenever you are struggling with uncertainty, worry, and anxiety.
*   Week 5—You will learn about centering prayer, which can help you yield to God's loving, active presence, beyond thoughts and feelings. Whenever you are feeling uncertain and anxious and worrying about tomorrow, centering prayer can help you to deepen your trust in God by letting go of control.
*   Week 6—You will continue with your daily practice of centering prayer, given that this type of contemplation is foundational to our program. In this week, you will learn about some of the contemplative attitudes that are cultivated in your solitude with God, shedding your own efforts to attain certainty and control because God is ministering to you within your unconscious.
*   Week 7—You will learn about the welcoming prayer, which is related to centering prayer. With the welcoming prayer, you will be learning to embrace your anxiety, inviting God into the experience. Over time, our hope is that you will be able to relate to your inner world with more

compassion and non-judgment, rather than trying to get rid of anxiety through the attainment of certainty and worry.

- Week 8—In the final week, you will review our Christian model of worry one last time, and learn a condensed version of contemplative practice to help you yield to God's active, loving presence during instances of doubt, uncertainty, worry, and anxiety. Given that you will be using contemplation beyond this program, you will learn about ways to prepare yourself for the road ahead.

Preparing for the Road Ahead: Practical Considerations

As you prepare for daily contemplative practice, we suggest that you try to carve out at least 20 to 40 minutes each day to spend with God. Certainly, one of the most important parts of this transition to daily solitude is the time commitment. In other words, you will have a wide variety of distractions, which capture the realities of life. Yet, setting aside this time for slowing down to sit at Jesus' feet is foundational, reminiscent of Mary in the gospel of Luke (10:38–42). Therefore, making the necessary adjustments beforehand is crucial.

Also, we encourage you to find the right location to practice contemplation. You might find a space in an extra bedroom of your home, or even use your parked car to create a silent, still space for practice. In either case, if possible, try to find a location that is free from distractions and excessive noise, given that silence and stillness are vital ingredients of the practice. To slow down requires that you are able to sink into the experience, rather than getting pulled away by the fast-paced world you are withdrawing from to find rest.

Overcoming Challenges

Because of the time commitment, you may find that it is difficult to press on, struggling to find the time to sit with God in silence. In fact, your mind might repeatedly tell you that this time spent with him is useless and that you have better things to do. Moreover, you might be incredibly tired from a long day, struggling to prioritize contemplative prayer as the most important task throughout your week. When these barriers arise, try to simply surrender them to God, recognizing that they will inevitably come.

With the actual practice, you are likely to experience a wide range of inner experiences, beyond the outer distractions of the world. For example, you may struggle with boredom or increased worry and anxiety. As you learn to settle in, you might find that you are increasingly aware of just how busy your mind can be. When you notice these inner experiences, try to apply an attitude of surrender, recognizing that your busy, anxious, and driven mind might never fully settle down. Reminiscent of an athlete with a nagging injury who repeatedly sees a physical therapist, you may need to reach out to God for his loving care in each moment in which you find yourself vulnerable to these distracting inner experiences; yet, over time, this reaching out to God, trusting in his providential care, can help you to find rest when the storms of the inner world continue to move through town.

Above all else, our hope is that you are able to patiently endure, remaining hopeful that God is active and moving in your life. Even though you might not "feel" better, this attitude of surrender that you will be cultivating can help you to deepen your trust in God, sitting at his feet no matter what inner events seem to arise. Whether you experience uncertainty, worry, or anxiety, our hope is that you develop the ability to pivot towards an awareness of God and find peace when the seas of the inner world have not fully settled.

The Serenity Prayer: Balancing Acceptance and Change by Turning to God

Before concluding this chapter, we would like to explore some of the central ingredients of the Serenity Prayer, a famous form of prayer that is often cited in the mindfulness-based literature in the field of clinical psychology. We believe that the Serenity Prayer, written by Reinhold Niebuhr some time ago, seems to best capture the most salient ingredients of the eight-week program that you are about to embark upon.

> God grant me the serenity to accept the things I cannot change; courage to change the things I can; and wisdom to know the difference. Living one day at a time; enjoying one moment at a time; accepting hardships as the pathway to peace; taking, as He did, this sinful world as it is, not as I would have it; trusting that He will make all things right if I surrender to His Will; that I may be reasonably happy in this life and supremely happy with Him forever in the next. Amen.

Within this quote, notice that there is an emphasis on accepting what cannot be changed, surrendering to God in each passing moment because he is benevolent and active. In fact, in this famous prayer, there seems to be an emphasis on trusting God, especially when you cannot change the hardships and suffering you will inevitably face in this world. Still, because Christians have hope, placing a firm trust in God's redemptive plan through Jesus' birth, life, death, and resurrection, you have the ability to balance acceptance and action. To follow Jesus, yielding to his plan for your life, means cultivating a deeper wisdom to know when to accept and when to change the inner and outer challenges you face on a daily basis. From our perspective, surrendering your inner world to God, especially your uncertainty, doubts, worry, and anxiety, is a fitting, effective alternative to trying to create a pseudo-sense of certainty on your own and in isolation.

Exercise: Writing Your Own Serenity Prayer to God

In this final exercise for the week, see if you can write your own Serenity Prayer to God, reminiscent of Niebuhr's inspirational quote. If possible, try to express a deeper desire to surrender to God, trusting that his infinite knowledge and wisdom, goodness and love, and presence and power will guide your paths from moment to moment. Letting go, try to express a willingness to "transfer the reins" to him. Begin a lifelong process of falling into his loving arms.

CONCLUSION

In the first week of the program, you were able to explore the link between uncertainty, worry, and anxiety, integrating a biblical viewpoint into this psychological understanding of chronic worry. As a Christian, a central part of your daily living likely involves trusting in God's plan for your life, yielding to his will, reminiscent of Jesus in the Garden of Gethsemane before his crucifixion (Luke 22:42). What is more, you began to explore the foundational tenets of contemplative practice, given that this form of Christian prayer can help you to let go of your own tendencies to control, predict, and plan each and every detail of the future. Because obtaining certainty is not humanly possible, learning to let go of your "approach" and "avoidance" strategies is especially important in order to find some relief from your suffering.

In the next chapter, you will continue to explore the main ingredients of contemplative practice, trying on this form of prayer on a daily basis. As you begin to sit in silence with God, our hope is that you will learn to pivot towards him during instances of uncertainty and doubt, trusting that he will provide for you because he is sovereign over all of creation. Because you believe in a personal God, it is important to remind yourself that he is active and present, loving you and caring for you with outstretched arms. Yet, to trust God on a much deeper level, we believe contemplative practice can help you by offering an experiential way of knowing what is beyond words.

REFERENCES

Dugas, M., & Robichaud, M. (2007). *Cognitive-Behavioral Treatment for Generalized Anxiety Disorder: From Science to Practice*. New York: Routledge.

Foster, R. (2001). *Streams of Living Water: Celebrating the Great Traditions of the Christian Faith*. New York: HarperCollins Publishers.

Keating, T. (2002). *Open Mind, Open Heart: The Contemplative Dimension of the Gospel*. New York: Continuum.

Knabb, J., Frederick, T., & Cumming, G. (2016). Surrendering to God's Providence: A Three-Part Study on Providence-Focused Therapy for Recurrent Worry (PFT-RW). *Psychology of Religion and Spirituality*. Advanced online publication.

Laird, M. (2006). *Into the Silent Land: A Guide to the Christian Practice of Contemplation*. New York: Oxford University Press.

Week 2

AN INTRODUCTION TO CONTEMPLATIVE PRACTICE

Introduction

In the second chapter, you will learn about the contemplative Christian tradition, which dates back to roughly the third century. This week, you will have the opportunity to explore the history of contemplation, the influence that *apophatic* prayer has had on contemplative Christianity, and key writings on the topic. Moreover, you will learn about the role that divine union, or *theosis*, may play in deepening your relationship with God, turning to him during instances of uncertainty, doubt, worry, and anxiety in order to surrender to his loving care. To conclude the chapter, you will begin daily contemplative prayer, practicing sitting in silence with God in order to transfer control to him.

A Brief History of Contemplative Christianity: Eastern and Western Influences

Starting around the third or fourth century, Christians began to move to the deserts of Egypt to let go of a preoccupation with worldly endeavors and to relinquish the grip that society had on them.[1] Within the hot, dry desert, these committed Christians longed to connect to God on a deeper level, facing their temptations as a way to draw closer to him. Further, they renounced the evils of society that frequently tested their loyalty to God (see 1 Peter and Revelation). In the process, they developed a unique way of understanding the inner world, reciting scripture (often the Psalms) as a strategy to focus their attention on God and pivot away from tempting thoughts (which they often attributed to demons).

Over time, these experiences were written down, converted into teachings within the *Sayings of the Desert Fathers*. At a certain point, desert monks began to shorten their prayers, which eventually led to the Jesus Prayer: "Lord Jesus Christ, Son of God, have mercy on me, a sinner." Focusing on a condensed phrase from scripture, these devoted Christians recognized the importance of sustained attention, given they frequently had to deal with boredom, sadness, and anxiety (among other distressing emotions) within the desert life. As they let go of their old patterns of living, there was most certainly a wide variety of inner experiences they had to face, such as a sense of loss, frustration about unmet physical or relational needs, and so on. Therefore, throughout the day, they needed to learn a new way to keep their attention on God and maintain stillness and silence, finding joy in the midst of difficult inner and outer experiences.

In fact, a foundational ingredient of daily life with God involved an attitude of "renunciation," or "freedom from care" (Burton-Christie, 1993). In other words, these desert residents actively turned to God to provide for them, shedding all unilateral attempts to create safety, security, predictability, and certainty about the future. Also referred to as "detachment" (Burton-Christie, 1993), the early desert Christians viewed an utter dependence on God as the ideal, relinquishing both inner and outer distractions, which they used to rely upon for daily living. Over time, this attitude of "detachment" and "renunciation" led to a sort of freedom, which helped them to focus exclusively on God's providence from moment to moment. Frequently, this detachment and renunciation led to living profoundly solitary lives so that monks could focus completely on their relationship with God. Certainly, though, there were setbacks, with monks often falling short of this lofty goal. These practices of renunciation and detachment, as well as other habits of early desert monks, offer Christians in the twenty-first century key psychospiritual tools for relating differently to inner distress. These tools can help you to enhance your connection to, and reliance on, God. At the same time, you will be learning to cope more effectively with persistent psychological struggles.

When the Catholic and Eastern Orthodox Church split around the turn of the second millennium, Catholics continued to write about the contemplative experience, anchored to the *Sayings of the Desert Fathers*. Examples of Western contemplative authors over the centuries include St. John of the Cross, Meister Eckhart, Julian of Norwich, and St. Theresa of Avila. What is more, the Eastern Orthodox Church compiled their experiences of contemplative prayer within the *Philokalia*, which is a collection of sayings on the contemplative life, turning to the Jesus Prayer to achieve divine union.

Within the twenty-first century, there has most certainly been a return to some of these contemplative influences within the Christian life, with the reemergence of contemplation in the form of the "prayer of the senses," the Jesus Prayer, centering prayer, the welcoming prayer, *lectio divina*, and so on. Interestingly, several of these vehicles through which divine union, or *theosis*, is pursued involve a wordless form of prayer, drawing from *apophatic* theology. Within the *apophatic* tradition, God is often viewed as *ineffable*, transcending our human ability to describe him with language. In other words, the *apophatic* tradition encourages our spiritual growth, helping us to rise above the limits of knowledge and words in order to gaze upon God's presence.

Wordless Prayer and the *Apophatic* Tradition

Within the *apophatic* tradition, or *via negativa*, it is impossible to fully wrap our minds around God, given that God is beyond mere human comprehension (see Egan, 1978). In other words, employing words, symbols, and images to understand God will ultimately fall short since God is so much more than these limiting forms of expression. On the other hand, the *kataphatic* tradition utilizes human words to describe God, pointing to both scripture and the incarnation as fitting examples of the use of language to capture God's attributes, qualities, and actions.

Characteristics of *apophatic* prayer (adapted from Lane, 1998):

- Sitting in silence in your time spent with God.
- Letting go of the tendency to use language in your time spent with God.
- Employing an attitude of mystery and awe in your time spent with God.
- Developing a loving attitude in your time spent with God.
- Letting go of control in your time spent with God.
- Emptying yourself in your time spent with God.

- Cultivating an attitude of vulnerability, humility, and surrender in your time spent with God.
- Relinquishing all expectations in your time spent with God.
- "Praying with your eyes shut" in your time spent with God (Peterson, 1989).

Characteristics of *kataphatic* prayer (adapted from Lane, 1998):

- Using language, thoughts, feelings, sensations, and images in your time spent with God.
- Using scripture in your time spent with God.
- Using metaphors to capture God's attributes in your time spent with God.
- "Praying with your eyes open" in your time spent with God (Peterson, 1989).

Over time, contemplatives began to turn to an *apophatic*, wordless form of prayer to deepen their relationship with God. Rather than using language as a vehicle through which they conversed with God, monks throughout the ages would sit in silence with God, letting go of their own cognitive efforts to understanding him. Instead, they believed that God was beyond words and images, leading to the desire to have a direct encounter with him. One such contemplative writing—*The Cloud of Unknowing*—was written in the fourteenth century, offering guidance on the use of *apophatic* prayer to rest in God's presence and deepen an intimate union with him.

We believe that *apophatic* prayer can be especially helpful in your struggle with uncertainty, doubt, worry, and anxiety. Based on its emphasis on wordless, imageless prayer, we argue that sitting with God in silence can help you let go of the tendency to use words to achieve a pseudo-sense of certainty. Stated differently, *apophatic* prayer can help you let go of the use of language to try to "fill in the gaps," predicting an uncertain future through the cognitive medium of worry.

Instead, during moments of contemplation, you are actually learning to let go of the tendency to overly rely on your mind's interpretation of uncertainty, pivoting towards a silent awareness of God's active, loving presence. Over time, we believe that *apophatic* prayer can help you to shift from a cognitive, worrying state to a restful, wordless fellowship with God. Relinquishing the grip you may have on worry, you might find that your time spent with God is nourishing and comforting because you are not lost in a sea of thoughts, images, and memories.

Of course, *kataphatic* prayer is also central in the Christian life. Yet, using words to understand God can be a form of gaining certainty about who God is and how God works in the world—another form of IU. Now, we are not arguing that the *kataphatic* tradition is wrong or unhelpful—clearly "the word of God is alive and active," "sharper than any double-edged sword" (Hebrews 4:12). However, we need to be attentive to our efforts to attain certainty in order to manage our anxieties, whether these anxieties are about physical or spiritual concerns. In fact, we will introduce you to a form of *kataphatic* prayer—the "prayer of the senses"—in the next chapter.

Nevertheless, during moments of *apophatic* contemplation, you will learn to sit with God, trusting in him without having to petition him for some sort of guaranteed outcome. Reminiscent of sitting with a loved one in silence while watching the sun set on the porch of your home, you might find that there are moments of formal and informal contemplative practice that involve letting go of your tendency to overly rely on worry to achieve a certain, predictable future. Because your main task is just to sit with God, like a loved one on the porch, you can allow your worrying mind to continue to do what it will do—generate thoughts. Still, when you notice that you have been distracted—pulled into an avalanche of worry—you can simply acknowledge the distraction before gently shifting your attention back to God's silent, loving presence.

THE CLOUD OF UNKNOWING[2]

In the fourteenth century, an anonymous monk in England wrote *The Cloud of Unknowing*, offering instructions on *apophatic* prayer as a way to help the reader understand the benefits of the contemplative life, including how to achieve them. Using the story in the gospel of Luke (10:38–42) about Jesus' visit to the home of Mary and Martha, *The Cloud* author argued that Mary captures the contemplative life. On the other hand, Martha embodies the active life. Both, of course, are integral parts of Christian living; yet, Mary's yielding, submissive posture can be especially important when considering healthy psychological and spiritual functioning among Christians with chronic worry. Specifically, she was able to gaze upon Jesus, placing him at the center of her world. Rather than getting bogged down with distractions, reminiscent of Martha, Mary listened to Jesus as she spent time with him.

In addition, *The Cloud* author used the image of a cloud to help the reader understand the importance of employing love, rather than knowledge, as a way to reach out to God. During contemplative practice, *The Cloud* author advocated for placing all distracting inner experiences (e.g., thoughts, feelings, sensations) underneath a "cloud of forgetting," looking up to God in love instead of knowledge. Gazing upon God, from *The Cloud* author's perspective, requires accepting that this loving, trusting lunge towards him will reach a point of uncertainty. In turn, God will be found in a dark cloud beyond words and images—*a cloud of unknowing*. In this moment, *apophatic* prayer involves relinquishing all human efforts to understand God (via self-derived knowledge, drawing from symbols, images, language, and so on), trusting that he is active and present. As *The Cloud* author revealed:

> The essence of contemplation is a simple and direct reaching out to God. People who pray at this depth do not seek relief from pain nor do they seek increased rewards, but only the fulfillment of God's will. Nothing else shares this simple moment. (quoted in Bangley, 2006, p. 37)

In these instances of contemplative practice, *The Cloud* author explained that a simple, single-syllable word can be used to focus on God, especially when practitioners are distracted with unruly thoughts, feelings, and sensations. In other words, since these thoughts (and other inner experiences) can get in the way of a direct experience of God, shifting your focus back to a short, simplistic word can help you to stay attentive to God's presence. The word, though, has no meaning, other than to symbolize your attentive gaze upon God, who resides in a dark *cloud of unknowing*. Over time, your loving movement towards God, employing a simple, short word, can help you to cultivate a deeper trust in him, pivoting towards God when you realize you are distracted with uncertainty, doubt, worry, and anxiety.

Above all else, this special time spent with God can help you to deepen your intimacy with him, beyond words and images that capture only a limited understanding of God. To have a direct encounter with him, perseverance is required, especially since the *cloud of unknowing* can be very difficult to face. This experience is consistent with developing a new relationship or attaining a new skillset, which usually increases anxiety. Certainly, it is only human nature to get distracted with thoughts, feelings, images, and memories, convincing yourself that these inner experiences are absolutely critical to your relationship with him. By relying on God's grace, though, you will be cultivating a deeper trust and union with him, as *The Cloud* author explained:

> If you sincerely turn from the world to God, trust that God will give you either everything you need, or the patience to endure without it. What difference does it make which of the two you have? (Bangley, 2006, p. 35)

With regular practice, contemplative prayer can start to feel incredibly familiar, reminiscent of sitting with the old friend on the porch and letting go of your own efforts to describe the experience with words, which only pull you away from a direct encounter in the moment. Before transitioning to the main ingredients in this eight-week program that we would like for you to take part in, we offer a brief overview of the notion of divine union, frequently discussed in the contemplative literature.

Divine Union and *Theosis*: Deepening Your Intimacy with God

Within the Greek Orthodox tradition, the foundational aim of the contemplative life is *theosis*, or "union with God" (Coniaris, 1998). Within the pages of the *Philokalia*, *theosis* is described over and over again, pointing the reader to this intimate closeness with God. As Coniaris revealed, the Christian experience is chiefly focused on participating in the life that God offers. Other ways to describe *theosis* are as follows (adapted from Coniaris, 1998):

- Entering into the life that God offers to Christians.
- Healing the *imago Dei* in Christians.
- Being an active participant in God's kingdom and love.
- Reconciling with God by way of divine union.
- Intimacy with Christ.

To cultivate *theosis*, the *Philokalia* encourages Christians to practice contemplative prayer, including the Jesus Prayer (which will be explored in a subsequent week of this program). In the meantime, though, just know that the contemplative tradition takes seriously the notion that Christians can deepen their intimacy with God, sharing in God's love and healing the inner world in the process.

Interestingly, there has even been a renewed interest in *theosis* among evangelical Christians (see Rakestraw, 1997). For Rakestraw, there are several examples in scripture that seem to capture this divine union illuminated in the *Philokalia*, including Genesis 1:26 and 2 Peter 1:3–4:

> Then God said, "Let us make mankind *in our image, in our likeness*, so that they may rule over the fish in the sea and the birds of the sky, over the livestock and all the wild animals, and over all the creatures that move along the ground." (italics added)
>
> His divine power has given us everything we need for a godly life through our knowledge of him who called us by his own glory and goodness. Through these he has given us his very great and precious promises, so that through them you may *participate in the divine nature*, having escaped the corruption in the world caused by evil desires. (italics added)

As these verses reveal, humankind was created in the "likeness" and "image" of God, with Christians literally partaking in God's "divine nature." According to Rakestraw, *theosis* can be formally defined as follows:

> In this life Christians grow more and more into the very likeness and character of God as God was revealed in the man Jesus Christ. (p. 261)

When thinking about *theosis*, it is important to consider God's intimate relationship with creation. "Communion with God is the goal of creation and salvation. The church calls this goal *christification* or, more commonly, deification (from the Greek *theosis*)" (Nassif, 2012, p. 53). As Christians practice listening to, and learning about, Christ, they resemble him more and more. That is, Christians increasingly participate in the life of Christ by praying more, ministering more, and loving more. In a very real way, Christ is the perfect human, and Christians participate in this true humanity by loving God and neighbor (Matthew 22:36–40; Nassif, 2012). Christlikeness means becoming more and more like Christ—within both the inner world and outer world. We learn to attend to God's active presence, resulting in more and more love for our neighbors.

Christ, as the divine Word, is the image of God that is present on this planet. Christ is all that Adam, the first human, is not (Hebrews 2–3). As Hebrews (2:9) affirms: "But we do see Jesus, who was made lower than the angels for a little while, now crowned with glory and honor because he suffered death, so that by the grace of God he might taste death for everyone." In Christ's glorification, he reconciles God to the human world. By being perfect, Christ is the realized image of God. Bonhoeffer (1997 [1959], p. 39) described the image of God in humans as follows:

> In man God creates his image on earth. This means that man is like the Creator in that he is free. Actually he is free only by God's creation, by means of the Word of God; he is free for the worship of the Creator.

Christ, in actuality of his being, is the only person truly free to worship God the Father in complete obedience. In other words, "[t]he Spirit of God mediates the reality of God to us through the humanity of Christ and, through that same humanity, mediates us to God" (Anderson, 1997, p. 74). Jesus Christ humanizes the Spirit of God (i.e., the incarnation), and he also humanizes humanity: "Through Jesus Christ we see the anger of God expressed at that which dehumanizes humanity, whether it be disease, demons, or misuse of the law itself" (Anderson, 1997, p. 76). As we become more and more like Christ, we experience transformation in action and experience.

In one of the earliest examples of a Christian hymn, Paul instructed us to have the same mindset as Christ (Philippians 2:5–11):

> In your relationships with one another, have the same mindset as Christ Jesus: Who, being in very nature God, did not consider equality with God something to be used to his own advantage; rather, he made himself nothing by taking the very nature of a servant, being made in human likeness. And being found in appearance as a man, he humbled himself by becoming obedient to death—even death on a cross! Therefore God exalted him to the highest place and gave him the name that is above every name, that at the name of Jesus every knee should bow, in heaven and on earth and under the earth, and every tongue acknowledge that Jesus Christ is Lord, to the glory of God the Father.

In this passage, Christ's mindset is characterized by humility and obedience. Therefore, Christians are to share these same attitudes. These inner qualities result in external action—we are to treat others as more important than ourselves. This passage emphasizes for us that being like Christ is both an activity for the mind as well as an action towards one's neighbors. Both the internal (or mind) and the external (or action) are important in becoming more Christlike.

We obey Christ more and more in being and doing. 1 Peter 1:13–21 reveals: (a) Christ's obedience to God; and (b) the glory that God gives to Christ for his righteous suffering. Christians are reminded of Christ "who through him [are believers] in God, who raised him from the dead and glorified him, so that your faith and hope are in God" (1 Peter 1:21). Christ's redemption (1 Peter 1:18–19) provides the faith and hope that God will vindicate his chosen people in the last days. At the same time, though, Christians are responsible to maintain their commitments to Christ and follow his example (Hillyer, 1992). What follows is our understanding of the main tenets of contemplative practice, focusing on the ultimate aim of intimacy with God, who heals and restores Christians to share in his love and bear his image.

An Integrative Understanding: The Central Ingredients of Contemplative Prayer

In our view, contemplative prayer is about sitting with God in silence, letting go of the tendency to use thoughts, feelings, and sensations to make sense of your relationship with him. Rather, through a deeper trust in his active, loving presence, you are learning to find rest in solitude with him. You are also slowing down from the busyness of the inner and outer world in order to cultivate sustained attention, gazing upon him with a loving attentiveness. Although using language is foundational in your prayer life as a Christian—after all, Jesus taught Christians how to pray using actual words (Luke 11:2–4)—we believe that contemplative prayer, drawing from the *apophatic* tradition, can help you to let go of the grip that thinking has on your inner world. Because your worrying thoughts can get in the way of a restful, loving gaze upon God, our hope is that daily contemplative practice can help you accomplish several tasks:

- Let go of the tendency to use cognition as a way to generate certainty, chronically worrying to "fill in the blanks" of an uncertain, unknown future.
- Relate to worrying thoughts with a bit more distance, gently noticing when they are present before returning to your loving gaze upon God.
- Slowly learn to trust in God's providence to guide your future paths, rather than employing worry to attain a certain future, which is not humanly possible.
- Partake in God's gift of love, moving towards healing and intimacy with God as you rest at his feet from moment to moment.

In order to accomplish these aims, we present several forms of contemplative practice in the next seven weeks, the majority of which are rooted in the *apophatic* tradition. Still, we also include a *kataphatic* form of prayer—the "prayer of the senses"—so that you can also utilize your God-given senses to relate to scripture in a fresh, new way. In either case, below are the contemplative practices you will be "trying on" over the course of the remaining weeks in this program.

Forms of Contemplative Prayer in this Workbook

Beginning this week, you will practice daily contemplation, which includes the following forms of prayer:

- Week 2—Contemplative prayer (adapted from Finley, 2004), focusing on the breath.
- Week 3—The "prayer of the senses" (Endean, 1990), focusing on the five senses to relate differently to a biblical story.
- Week 4—The "Jesus Prayer" (Talbot, 2013), focusing on repeating the phrase, "Lord Jesus Christ, Son of God, have mercy on me, a sinner."
- Week 5—"Centering prayer" (Keating, 2006), focusing on using "surrender" as your prayer word.
- Week 6—Continuing with "centering prayer" (Frenette, 2012), with "surrender" as the prayer word.

- Week 7—The "welcoming prayer" (Bourgeault, 2004), learning to embrace your inner pain, invite God into the process, and surrender your desire to control or get rid of the pain to God.
- Week 8—"Three-minute breathing with Jesus" (adapted from Segal et al., 2012), which can help you to use contemplative prayer throughout your day, beyond your formal practice.

Letting Go of Uncertainty and Worry: Contemplation and Yielding to God's Providence

Within each of these forms of contemplative prayer, our hope is that you will move in the direction of letting go of your control efforts, which have likely failed to create certainty in your life. These efforts also include cognitive attempts to use knowledge to gain certainty, especially certainty in your relationship with God. Instead, as you learn to slow down enough to sit in silence with God, you may find that you are able to deepen your awareness of his active, loving presence, yielding to his will because you are fortifying your relationship with him. As you rest in his arms, you might be able to relinquish your need for certainty, trusting in God's providential care in the process. Because he is all-knowing, all-loving, and all-powerful, pivoting away from your distracting, worrying thoughts and towards his loving embrace is key. In other words, you are letting go of your need to "know," for certain, what the future will hold. You are also reaching out to him in love as his grace and mercy help you to heal in your ability to bear his image.

Contemplative Prayer in Daily Life

As you prepare to start daily contemplative practice, we would like to explore some of the potential barriers that can get in the way of devoting 20-minute blocks of time to yielding to God's active, loving presence. First, contemplative prayer may feel very foreign to you as you get started. Given we live in a fast-paced society, you might find that you have a hard time being still during these longer periods of time spent with God. In fact, you may quickly recognize that your relationship with God has historically consisted of *you* talking to God, praying to God, and reading your Bible—all cognitive, language-based endeavors. As you enter into a wordless, imageless time spent with him, it may be hard to trust that he is there. When these doubts come up, our hope is that you will surrender them, too, given that God is active and present in your life. In other words, he is a personal God who loves you, wanting nothing more than to spend these silent, still moments with you as you sit at his feet.

Moreover, you may find that there seems to be little time in daily living to focus on silent, still meditation. To be certain, you may notice that the quiet time you spend with God seems to be less important than other tasks at the top of your "to-do list." When your mind begins to convince you that these 20 minutes per day are not really important, try to allow these thoughts to just run their natural course, without fully buying into them. When you notice them, just return to your focus on God, captured in your breath or a prayer word. To be sure, not only are the *minutes* per day important, getting into the habit of silent, wordless prayer on a *daily basis* is important, too. As a result, as best you can, try to focus on consistency, even when you are having trouble finding the time. Recognize that you are learning a new way of relating to the inner world, inviting God into the process to "transfer the reins" to him.

In your relationships, too, you may notice that others are not fully supportive of your time in solitude with God. If this happens, try to offer compassion to others, recognizing that they are concerned that they are missing out on the time they would otherwise spend with you. Yet, given that these moments of silent contemplation are essential to healthy psychological and spiritual functioning, try to continue to carve out this important time with God.

Finally, as you learn new ways—via contemplative practice—to relinquish your desire to control, plan, and predict your future with absolute certainty, your worrying thoughts and anxious feelings may continue to surface. In fact, you might notice that your worry seems to intensify in its frequency and duration, especially when you let go of the grip you have on it. If this happens, try to apply an attitude of surrender and trust to these thoughts, too, inviting God into the process and trusting that he is in control. After all, he is all-knowing, all-loving, and all-powerful.

EXERCISE: 20 MINUTES OF CONTEMPLATIVE PRAYER

In this exercise, which is adapted from Finley's (2004) and Segal et al.'s (2012) recommendations, please get into a comfortable position, planning on 20 minutes of silent, wordless prayer. In this time, you will want to find a comfortable chair in a quiet environment, free from distractions. You can start by listening to the audio file (Track 1 at https://www.routledge.com/Contemplative-Prayer-for-Christians-with-Chronic-Worry-An-Eight-Week-Program/Knabb-Frederick/p/book/9781138690943 under the eResource tab) that accompanies this book, eventually learning how to enter into this time on your own.

- When you are ready, get into a comfortable position, closing your eyes and saying a brief prayer to God. "Father, in the next 20 minutes, I am surrendering my inner world to you, letting go of my own efforts to control or predict my future by striving for absolute certainty. Instead, I am giving over my thoughts, feelings, and sensations to you, with my breath serving as a symbol of this yielding, consenting attitude of surrender. I pray that you are with me, guiding this process as I repeatedly surrender to you."
- Now, begin to notice that you are breathing, paying attention to your breath in a specific location throughout the cycle. You might want to focus on the air going in and out of your nostrils, or your abdomen expanding and constricting. In either case, pay close attention to the reality that you do not need to control your breathing in any way. Instead, God is controlling your breath, offering you the "breath of life." As you gently inhale and exhale, let go of your own efforts to control the process, trusting that God is sustaining you by controlling your breathing.
- Continue to sink further and further into this reality, letting go of all your own efforts with each breath. Since God is active and present, there is nothing you need to be doing, other than focusing on his gift—your breath going in and out of your lungs. Repeatedly, let go of the tendency to want to think or feel a certain way, recognizing that God is completely and totally sovereign. He is loving you and offering you grace and mercy as he interacts with you in a personal, life-giving manner.
- At a certain point, you will recognize that you are distracted by a thought or feeling. When this happens—it is inevitable—just notice the thought or feeling that has pulled you away from your breathing. After briefly labeling the thought or feeling, such as "worry" or "anxiety," compassionately return to your breathing, noticing that your inner experiences wax and wane from moment to moment.
- As you continue to notice your breathing, apply an attitude of non-judgment to the process, recognizing that God is all you need in this very moment. He loves you and is sustaining you, offering you the "breath of life." Therefore, there is nothing else you need to be doing in this very moment. There is no need to think about the future or

anticipate what lies ahead. Rather, since God is pursuing you and loving you in the here and now, with your best intentions in mind, you can rest at his feet.

- Now that this exercise has come to a close, try to sit in silence for a minute, before giving thanks to God for this time spent with him. See if you can apply this attitude of surrender to God throughout your day.

Once you have completed this 20-minute exercise, see if you can write down some of your thoughts about the initial experience. What was it like? What, if anything, got in the way of sitting in silence with God? Were you able to gently return to your breath when you recognized you were worrying or feeling anxious? How can you continue to apply this attitude of surrender to the rest of your day, trusting that God is active and present as he loves you and sustains you with his providential care?

_____

_____

_____

_____

_____

_____

_____

EXERCISE: RECORDING YOUR DAILY EFFORTS

Beyond briefly writing about the initial experience (completed above), each day, see if you can record your efforts, jotting down some of your reactions to the practice after you have concluded each 20-minute session.

Day of the Week	Length of Time Practiced (Minutes)	Experience of Uncertainty, Doubt, Worry, and Anxiety Before and After the Practice	Experience of God's Active, Loving Presence Before and After the Practice	Inner Barriers to Contemplative Practice (Thoughts, Feelings, and Sensations)	Outer Barriers to Contemplative Practice (Environmental Distractions)
Monday					
Tuesday					
Wednesday					

AN INTRODUCTION TO CONTEMPLATIVE PRACTICE

Thursday					
Friday					
Saturday					
Sunday					

EXERCISE: JOURNALING ABOUT YOUR EXPERIENCE

In the space that follows, see if you can journal about your experience of daily contemplative practice, beyond simply noting some of the reactions from the practice (which you were able to do in the section above). You might want to reflect on your experience with God, as well as your experience of uncertainty, doubt, worry, and anxiety before and after the practice. Again, use this space to dig a bit deeper, moving beyond brief descriptions of the experience of contemplative practice.

Monday

Tuesday

33

Wednesday

Thursday

Friday

AN INTRODUCTION TO CONTEMPLATIVE PRACTICE

Saturday

Sunday

Exercise: Homework for the Week

1. Practice the above 20-minute contemplative exercise at least once per day for the entire week.
2. Journal for at least 10 minutes per day about your contemplative exercise, focusing on what the experience was like and any potential barriers (e.g., thoughts, feelings, sensations) to focusing on your breathing (see above).
3. At least three times per day, try to notice God's presence, extending your formal practice to daily life.

Struggling with Contemplative Prayer: Perspectives from Erin, Ryan, and Lisa

In the second week of the program, Erin began to sit in silence with God on a daily basis. At first, she was extremely uncomfortable with the experience, given that she used control so often in her daily life. In the first few days, she noticed that she began to worry even more, wondering what might happen if she let go of her own efforts to predict an uncertain future. In fact, Erin recognized just how anxious she was about leaning on God for guidance, struggling to trust that he would work things out for the best. Mid-week, though, she began to look forward to sitting with God in silence, recalling how she used to get extremely excited to learn about Jesus in Sunday School. Although her worry and anxiety most certainly did not go away in her first week of contemplative practice, she did have brief moments of success, letting go of the grip she had on worry for short periods of time.

For Ryan, contemplative practice started out rather rough. As he would settle down to sit with God in silence, beyond words, he found that he had a very difficult time letting go. In fact, he felt tightness in his chest as he sat alone in the spare bedroom of his home for 20 minutes at a time. Each passing moment seemed to go on forever, with Ryan wondering what might happen if he stopped his efforts to gain control over an ambiguous future. As he endured this struggle, he started to notice on his fifth or sixth day that he had been battling with God, engaging in a sort of tug-of-war. Towards the end of the week, he started to "let go of the rope," briefly experiencing an inner freedom as he simply noticed his worrying thoughts and anxious feelings. On the seventh day, he had a very short moment that involved complete and total surrender to God, before he quickly reestablished his pseudo-grip on his future. Still, this short moment helped him to recognize that it might be possible—with time—to learn to trust God again, especially in his protective care. He might actually be able to let go of his own efforts to attain a certain future. Reflecting back on his relationship with God prior to his painful breakup, he recalled finding freedom in knowing that God would guide his paths. At the end of the second week, he longed to return to this relationship with God, filled with peace and comfort.

In Lisa's first day of contemplative prayer, she recognized that she had a hard time sitting alone with God. Possibly due to her family-of-origin experience, she seemed to dread taking the time to carve out solitude with God, filled with silence, stillness, and inactivity on her part. In her first few attempts to simply rest in God's presence, trying to deepen her intimacy with him, she felt especially anxious, recalling how hurt she felt when she learned of her husband's passing. Still, as she "stayed the course," continuing to return to solitude with God on a daily basis, she discovered there were moments that involved letting go and surrendering her inner world to God. Although she continued to struggle with uncertainty and doubt, by the end of the second week she discovered that she did have the ability to loosen the grip that worry had on her life, finding glimpses of freedom from her preoccupation with uncertainty and ambiguity.

In each of these cases, the participants continued to struggle with uncertainty, worry, and anxiety. Yet, they all decided to press on, recognizing the importance of spending time alone with God and surrendering to his loving arms. Although they most certainly did not achieve some sort of enlightened state—free from pain—the repeated shift towards the breath to symbolize God's active, loving presence helped them begin to recognize the importance of yielding to him.

CONCLUSION

In this chapter, you were introduced to the contemplative Christian tradition, including its desert roots, as well as concepts such as *apophatic* prayer and divine union. This week, our hope is that you were able to begin a lifelong journey of returning to God each and every time you notice that your mind has convinced you that attaining certainty, on your own, is absolutely essential. As you continue to sit with God, in silence and stillness, we believe you will move towards cultivating an attitude of surrender, which can be helpful in your efforts to let go of the grip you have on worry and the attainment of a certain, predictable future. In the third week of the program, you will learn about a *kataphatic* form of prayer to help you in your time of uncertainty, doubt, and worry, embedding yourself in Jesus' famous sermon on worry in order to spend time with him and develop a deeper union with your creator.

NOTES

1   For a detailed review of the history of the contemplative tradition, including its desert roots, see Burton-Christie (1993) and Farag (2012).
2   The following review of the actual text of *The Cloud of Unknowing* is drawn from Bangley's (2006) English translation. For a more scholarly review of the text, see Johnston (2000).

REFERENCES

Anderson, R. (1997). *The Soul of Ministry*. Louisville, KY: John Knox Press.
Bangley, B. (2006). *The Cloud of Unknowing: Contemporary English Edition*. Brewster, MA: Praclete Press.
Bonhoeffer, D. (1997 [1959]). *Creation and Fall/Temptation: Two Biblical Studies*. New York: Simon & Schuster.
Bourgeault, C. (2004). *Centering Prayer and Inner Awakening*. New York: Cowley Publications.
Burton-Christie, D. (1993). *The Word in the Desert: Scripture and the Quest for Holiness in Early Christian Monasticism*. New York: Oxford University Press.
Coniaris, A. (1998). *Philokalia: The Bible of Orthodox Spirituality*. Minneapolis, MN: Light & Life Publishing Company.
Egan, H. (1978). Christian Apophatic and Kataphatic Mysticisms. *Theological Studies, 39*, 399–426.
Endean, P. (1990). The Ignatian Prayer of the Senses. *The Heythrop Journal, 31*, 391–418.
Farag, L. (2012). *Balance of the Heart: Desert Spirituality for Twenty-First-Century Christians*. Eugene, OR: Cascade Books.
Finley, J. (2004). *Christian Meditation: Experiencing the Presence of God*. New York: HarperCollins Publishers.
Frenette, D. (2012). *The Path of Centering Prayer: Deepening Your Experience of God*. Boulder, CO: Sounds True, Inc.
Hillyer, N. (1992). *1 and 2 Peter, Jude*. Peabody, MA: Hendrickson Publishers.
Johnston, W. (2000). *The Mysticism of the Cloud of Unknowing*. New York: Fordham University Press.
Keating, T. (2006). *Open Mind, Open Heart, 20th Anniversary Edition*. New York: Continuum.
Lane, B. (1998). *The Solace of Fierce Landscapes: Exploring Desert and Mountain Spirituality*. New York: Oxford University Press.
Nassif, B. (2012). Orthodox Spirituality: A Quest for Transfigured Humanity. In B. Demarest (Ed.), *Four Views on Christian Spirituality* (pp. 27–59). Grand Rapids, MI: Zondervan.

Peterson, E. (1989). *The Contemplative Pastor: Returning to the Art of Spiritual Direction.* Grand Rapids, MI: William B. Eerdmans Publishing Company.

Rakestraw, R. (1997). Becoming like God: An Evangelical Doctrine of Theosis. *Journal of the Evangelical Theological Society, 40,* 257–269.

Segal, Z., Williams, M., & Teasdale, J. (2012). *Mindfulness-Based Cognitive Therapy for Depression* (2nd ed.). New York: The Guilford Press.

Talbot, J. (2013). *The Jesus Prayer: A Cry for Mercy, a Path of Renewal.* Downers Grove, IL: InterVarsity Press.

WEEK 3

IGNATIAN PRAYER

INTRODUCTION

In the third chapter, you will focus on Ignatian spirituality, including several *kataphatic* forms of prayer that we believe can help you with uncertainty and worry. Within the Jesuit contemplative tradition, there is an emphasis on God's presence, recognizing that God is active and responsive in daily living. Rather than keeping his distance, God is rooted in the present moment, interacting with you as you place one foot in front of the other on the roads of life. In fact, God is active not only in the mind but in the heart. This type of prayer also focuses on our experiences of God's active presence. Therefore, with this understanding in mind, Ignatian prayer can be helpful in allowing you to find God in each unfolding minute of the day, reaching out to him to guide your life, especially during instances of uncertainty, doubt, worry, and anxiety.

CHARACTERISTICS OF IGNATIAN SPIRITUALITY

Several centuries ago, Ignatius Loyola founded the Society of Jesus, or Jesuits, focusing on a variety of spiritual exercises in order to identify God's active, loving presence in daily life. In his most famous work, *Spiritual Exercises*, he outlined several different ways to cultivate a more receptive, open posture towards God (Jackson, n.d.). The *Spiritual Exercises* actually emphasize both meditation and contemplation for students of this famous teaching (Ignatian Spirituality, n.d.). Meditation in this sense is connected with the mind. Meditation is about reflecting on our thoughts and principles, using cognition in the process. Contemplation, on the other hand, is connected with the heart, drawing from imagination to deepen our experience of God. The role of imagination in Ignatian spirituality will be developed more in the "prayer of the senses." In fact, threaded throughout the four-week *Spiritual Exercises* program is a plethora of salient themes (Fink, 2001):

- God is the author of all of creation; as a result, it is important for Christians to cultivate a deeper appreciation for him, including his gifts.
- God is present, actively intervening in our daily functioning.
- In each passing moment, God gives himself to his creation.
- Even in the midst of suffering, God is active and present, loving his creation.

39

For the purpose of our program, we believe that the above elements of Ignatian spirituality are especially relevant, given that God reveals himself to his creation from moment to moment, offering a loving response even when you may be feeling uncertainty, worry, and anxiety. In other words, in the midst of your anxiety, God is offering you his love. He is actively working in your life to reveal his will.

Interestingly, Ignatius offered the following prayer, which we believe fully captures the ability to surrender to God's providential care, ameliorating uncertainty and worry in the process:

> Take, Lord, and receive all my liberty, my memory, understanding, my entire will, all that I have and call my own. You have given all to me. To you, Lord, I return it. Do with it as you will. Give me only your love and your grace: that is enough for me. (quoted in Jackson, n.d.)

In this program, though, see if you can substitute some of the more general language in his prayer with your current struggle with worry, uncertainty, and anxiety.

> Lord, take all of my uncertainty, worry, doubt, and anxiety. You have given everything to me. To you, Lord, I return everything, even when I do not know what the future will hold. Do with my thoughts and feelings as you will. Do with my possessions, relationships, and life circumstances as you will. Give me only your love and your grace: that is enough for me, even when I am uncertain, worrying, and anxious about an unknown future. (adapted from Jackson, n.d.)

Notice, here, that the most important part of Ignatius' prayer is to surrender everything to God, including both your inner world and your life circumstances. Because God is all-knowing, all-loving, and all-powerful, you can safely give to him everything that he already owns.

In picking up the role of contemplation and imagination, it is important to remember Foster's (2011) discussion on the imagination, sanctified by God. That is, our imaginations are important aspects of being made in God's image (*imago Dei*), along with the rest of our God-given psychological makeup—our ability to use rational thought, feel emotions, exert our will, and exhibit intentional, goal-directed behavior. In Ignatian spirituality, contemplation allows us to imagine ourselves in the biblical scene. Using meditative Bible reading (*lectio divina*), we are presented with a text. Engaging our imaginations allows us to actually enter the text—for example, picturing ourselves with Jesus during the Sermon on the Mount (Matthew 5) or as part of the crowd of five thousand that Jesus fed (Matthew 14:13–21). This use of our imagination allows us to change our heart, as well as our head.

"Prayer of the Senses"

Within our program, Ignatius' second week of *Spiritual Exercises* will be used to cultivate a deeper relationship with Christ. You will be meditating on his life, including his teaching on the relationship between worry and God's providence. In particular, you will be learning about and practicing the "prayer of the senses," which requires that you use all five senses—sight, sound, taste, touch, and smell—to actually embed yourself in a gospel story (Hansen, 2012). By immersing yourself in a biblical narrative, you will have the opportunity to actually talk to Jesus, interacting with him as you experience the Bible in a new, vibrant manner.

Before beginning the "prayer of the senses," it is important to prepare for the meditation. To begin, we need to collect ourselves, settling into the practice (Foster, 2011). This means that we need to let go of all the inner distractions and prepare to experience God in the text, interacting with God's word on a deeper level. We let go of our inner distress—including difficult thoughts, feelings, and sensations—because God is in control of our lives, especially our intrapsychic experiences. We are certain that God loves us, and that God has our best interests in mind. We do not need to create certainty in our ability to attain a specific future.

There are several key ingredients within the "prayer of the senses," including: (a) identifying a story within the gospels to meditate on for a period of time; (b) praying that God will guide the process, inviting him into the experience in order to learn from him and identify key questions you would like to ask him; (c) utilizing the five senses to include yourself in a biblical story, culminating with a conversation with Jesus, focused on asking him the previously identified question from your prayer time with God; and (d) waiting upon Jesus for a reply, listening intently to him as you spend time with him in the biblical story (Hansen, 2012).

In the space below, spend some time reading about Jesus' teaching on worry (Matthew 6:25–34). From there, see if you can write down a question or two that you would like to ask Jesus after spending time with God, asking him to reveal the most salient questions that are helpful in this moment to guide your journey. Finally, you will enter into a 20-minute exercise to experience the meditative practice.

> Therefore I tell you, do not worry about your life, what you will eat or drink; or about your body, what you will wear. Is not life more than food, and the body more than clothes? Look at the birds of the air; they do not sow or reap or store away in barns, and yet your heavenly Father feeds them. Are you not much more valuable than they? Can any one of you by worrying add a single hour to your life? And why do you worry about clothes? See how the flowers of the field grow. They do not labor or spin. Yet I tell you that not even Solomon in all his splendor was dressed like one of these. If that is how God clothes the grass of the field, which is here today and tomorrow is thrown into the fire, will he not much more clothe you—you of little faith? So do not worry, saying, "What shall we eat?" or "What shall we drink?" or "What shall we wear?" For the pagans run after all these things, and your heavenly Father knows that you need them. But seek first his kingdom and his righteousness, and all these things will be given to you as well. Therefore do not worry about tomorrow, for tomorrow will worry about itself. Each day has enough trouble of its own.

Now, see if you can spend some time with God, asking him to reveal one or two key questions you should ask Jesus when you enter into the "prayer of the senses." If possible, write your two questions below:

1. _____

_____

2. _____

_____

EXERCISE: 20-MINUTE "PRAYER OF THE SENSES" MEDITATION

For this exercise, please find a comfortable chair, free from distractions and excessive noise. Try to complete the exercise in at least 20 minutes. If you would like, you can follow along with the audio recording that is provided (Track 2 at https://www.routledge.com/Contemplative-Prayer-for-Christians-with-Chronic-Worry-An-Eight-Week-Program/Knabb-Frederick/p/book/9781138690943 under the eResource tab).

- To begin, please close your eyes and get in a comfortable position in your chair. Now, gently recite the prayer of contemplation from Ignatius' *Spiritual Exercises*: "Take, Lord, and receive all my liberty, my memory, understanding, my entire will, all that I have and call my own. You have given all to me. To you, Lord, I return it. Do with it as you will. Give me only your love and your grace: that is enough for me" (quoted in Jackson, n.d.).
- Next, begin to see Jesus as he is teaching the Sermon on the Mount in the first century A.D. A crowd has gathered as he is sharing his teachings on topics such as giving to the needy, prayer, and fasting. The hillside is green and spacious, with grass and wildflowers blowing in the wind. The sun is shining, and there is a light breeze in the air. As you listen to Jesus' powerful voice, you can see the Sea of Galilee off in the distance, radiating a bright blue color in the sunlight. Immerse yourself in this landscape, imagining that you are there among first-century Jews listening to Jesus of Nazareth.
- Jesus starts to teach about worry, in a gentle, confident voice. "Therefore I tell you, do not worry about your life, what you will eat or drink; or about your body, what you will wear. Is not life more than food, and the body more than clothes?" Feel your feet on the grass as you listen to his words. See the sunlight shining on the Sea of Galilee, and notice that you are in the presence of your Lord and Savior. Sense the energy among the crowd as you listen, firsthand, to his words on "worry."
- Jesus continues: "Look at the birds of the air; they do not sow or reap or store away in barns, and yet your heavenly Father feeds them. Are you not much more valuable than they? Can any one of you by worrying add a single hour to your life?" Hear the birds as Jesus points to God's active role in their life. Watch them effortlessly fly through the air.
- Jesus goes on: "And why do you worry about clothes? See how the flowers of the field grow. They do not labor or spin. Yet I tell you that not even Solomon in all his splendor was dressed like one of these. If that is how God clothes the grass of the field, which is here today and tomorrow is thrown into the fire, will he not much more clothe you—you of little faith?" Smell the wildflowers and grass blowing in the wind as Jesus points his finger in their direction. See their beauty as you fully surrender to Jesus' teaching, trusting that he is offering you true peace through this lesson on God's protective care.
- "So do not worry, saying, 'What shall we eat?' or 'What shall we drink?' or 'What shall we wear?' For the pagans run after all these things, and your heavenly Father knows that you need them. But seek first his kingdom and his righteousness, and all these things will be given to you as well. Therefore do not worry about tomorrow, for tomorrow will worry about itself. Each day has enough trouble of its own." Feel your way into Jesus' powerful declaration. Experience a deep trust in Jesus' words as he confidently assures you that God knows what you need and will provide for you.
- As Jesus concludes his sermon, imagine that you are able to approach him and talk to him about your struggles with worry and uncertainty. In other words, you are face to face with Jesus. Imagine looking into his eyes and being reassured that God is active in your life and caring for each and every one of your concerns. At this time, you can also ask him the questions you identified and wrote down in the earlier section. Wait to hear what he says to you about your unique experience of worry and uncertainty, as well as how he responds to your questions. Thank Jesus, embracing him as you surrender to God's providential care. Feel his loving arms, trusting in his words and presence.

Once you have completed this 20-minute exercise for the first time, see if you can write down some of your thoughts about the experience. What was it like? What, if anything, got in the way of using your senses to experience Jesus' teaching on worry? Were you able to return to the biblical scene when you recognized you were worrying or feeling anxious? How can you continue to apply this experience to the rest of your day, trusting that God is active and present as he loves you and sustains you with his providential care?

EXERCISE: RECORDING YOUR DAILY EFFORTS FOR THE "PRAYER OF THE SENSES"

In the space that follows, see if you can briefly document your daily experience of the "prayer of the senses" (beyond what you have documented in the space above).

Day of the Week	Length of Time Practiced (Minutes)	Experience of Uncertainty, Doubt, Worry, and Anxiety Before and After the Exercise	Experience of God's Active, Loving Presence Before and After the Exercise	Inner Barriers to the "Prayer of the Senses" (Thoughts, Feelings, and Sensations)	Outer Barriers to the "Prayer of the Senses" (Distractions in the Environment)
Monday					
Tuesday					
Wednesday					
Thursday					
Friday					
Saturday					
Sunday					

EXERCISE: JOURNALING ABOUT YOUR EXPERIENCE OF THE "PRAYER OF THE SENSES"

In the space that follows, see if you can journal about your experience of the "prayer of the senses" on a daily basis (beyond what you have documented in the space above). You might want to reflect on your experience with God, as well as your experience of uncertainty, doubt, worry, and anxiety before and after the practice. Remember to focus on how you see, hear, feel, smell, and taste this imaginative experience. Again, use this space to dig a bit deeper.

Monday

Tuesday

IGNATIAN PRAYER

Wednesday

Thursday

Friday

Saturday

Sunday

THE DAILY EXAMEN

Another active approach to noticing God is the use of the daily examen. Within Ignatius' *Spiritual Exercises*, he outlined the "daily examen," which typically involves prayerful reflection sometime around noon, as well as a similar approach at nighttime, looking back on the day's events to recognize God's active, loving presence. The examen allows us to recognize God in the daily grind, where we are mostly preoccupied with other things. The main ingredients of the examen are as follows (adapted from Ignatian Spirituality, n.d.):

- Recognizing God's active, loving presence throughout your day.
- Reflecting on the events of the day with a sense of thankfulness and appreciation, noticing God within your conversations, tasks, and activities.
- Connecting to your emotions, attempting to better understand what God was trying to reveal to you in your inner experiences (rather than automatically assuming that you need to get rid of them).
- Trying to identify a specific event throughout your day, asking God to reveal himself in the situation.
- Envisioning what tomorrow is going to look like, asking God to guide your paths as you navigate tomorrow's terrain.

Interestingly, this unique form of prayer was likely inspired by Psalm 139 (see Warner, 2010), which was written by David and is presented below:

> You have searched me, Lord, and you know me. You know when I sit and when I rise; you perceive my thoughts from afar. You discern my going out and my lying down; you are familiar with all my ways. Before a word is on my tongue you, Lord, know it completely. You hem me in behind and before, and you lay your hand upon me. Such knowledge is too wonderful for me, too lofty for me to attain. Where can I go from your Spirit? Where can I flee from your presence? If I go up to the heavens, you are there; if I make my bed in the depths, you are there. If I rise on the wings of the dawn, if I settle on the far side of the sea, even there your hand will guide me, your right hand will hold me fast. If I say, "Surely the darkness will hide me and the light become night around me," even the darkness will not be dark to you; the night will shine like the day, for darkness is as light to you. For you created my inmost being; you knit me together in my mother's womb. I praise you because I am fearfully and wonderfully made; your works are wonderful, I know that full well. My frame was not hidden from you when I was made in the secret place, when I was woven together in the depths of the earth. Your eyes saw my unformed body; all the days ordained for me were written in your book before one of them came to be. How precious to me are your thoughts, God! How vast is the sum of them! Were I to count them, they would outnumber the grains of sand—when I awake, I am still with you. If only you, God, would slay the wicked! Away from me, you who are bloodthirsty! They speak of you with evil intent; your adversaries misuse your name. Do I not hate those who hate you, Lord, and abhor those who are in rebellion against you? I have nothing but hatred for them; I count them my enemies. Search me, God, and know my heart; test me and know my anxious thoughts. See if there is any offensive way in me, and lead me in the way everlasting.

We believe that this passage can be especially helpful for you as you struggle with uncertainty and worry, given that David seemed to highlight that God is active, present, and omniscient.

Imagine this scene from David's life: Saul recruited David to fight the Philistines, who were causing all sorts of trouble (1 Samuel 16). David did many amazing things for the Lord on Saul's behalf. David slayed a giant Philistine that none of Saul's soldiers would face. David was the only one able to soothe Saul (with his lyre) when an evil spirit seemed to be tormenting him.

After one such encounter, David was again soothing Saul when Saul tried to stab him with a spear. David was able to escape, but Saul sent his soldiers to kill David at his own house (1 Samuel 19). Imagine that the King was trying to kill you. How would your body feel? What sensations would you experience? What would you be thinking?

David composed Psalm 59 (1–17):

Deliver me from my enemies, O God; be my fortress against those who are attacking me. Deliver me from evildoers and save me from those who are after my blood. See how they lie in wait for me! Fierce men conspire against me for no offense or sin of mine, Lord. I have done no wrong, yet they are ready to attack me. Arise to help me; look on my plight! You, Lord God Almighty, you who are the God of Israel, rouse yourself to punish all the nations; show no mercy to wicked traitors. They return at evening, snarling like dogs, and prowl about the city. See what they spew from their mouths—the words from their lips are sharp as swords, and they think, "Who can hear us?" But you laugh at them, Lord; you scoff at all those nations. You are my strength, I watch for you; you, God, are my fortress, my God on whom I can rely. God will go before me and will let me gloat over those who slander me. But do not kill them, Lord our shield, or my people will forget. In your might uproot them and bring them down. For the sins of their mouths, for the words of their lips, let them be caught in their pride. For the curses and lies they utter, consume them in your wrath, consume them till they are no more. Then it will be known to the ends of the earth that God rules over Jacob. They return at evening, snarling like dogs, and prowl about the city. They wander about for food and howl if not satisfied. But I will sing of your strength, in the morning I will sing of your love; for you are my fortress, my refuge in times of trouble. You are my strength, I sing praise to you; you, God, are my fortress, my God on whom I can rely.

When comparing the context of David's life—being pursued by Saul and his men—and this Psalm, what do you feel? What are you thinking? What are you experiencing?

Because God is all-knowing, all-loving, and all-powerful, you can trust that he is with you in the midst of your pain, guiding your paths, even when you do not know what lies ahead. In the exercise below, you will be guided through these five steps, which are adapted so that you can benefit from God's active presence in the midst of daily uncertainty, doubt, worry, and anxiety. If you can, try to reflect on your reactions to these steps twice per day over the course of the next week.

EXERCISE: RECOGNIZING GOD'S PRESENCE WITH THE DAILY EXAMEN

If you can, try to pause at noon and during the nighttime in order to examine your day, looking for ways in which God was active and present in the midst of your inner pain (adapted from Ignatian Spirituality, n.d.).

- Recognize God's active, loving presence throughout your day, especially when you are experiencing uncertainty and worrying about what will come next. Try to notice God's presence, asking how he is intervening in the midst of the ambiguity.
- When you are experiencing uncertainty and anxiety and worrying about an unknown future, try to give thanks to God. Recognize all of the ways he has blessed you as he interacts with you in the present moment.

- Connect to your uncertainty, doubt, worry, and anxiety, asking what God is revealing to you in these painful moments. Rather than dismissing them, see if you can better understand how God is working within these difficult inner experiences.
- Try to identify a specific event during your day, especially when you are feeling anxious, asking God to reveal himself in the situation.
- Envision what tomorrow is going to look like; however, instead of worrying about an uncertain future, ask God to give you strength and hope. Ask him to reveal himself so that you can cultivate a sense of peace in knowing he is all-knowing, all-loving, and all-powerful.

Although you will not be formally documenting this experience throughout your week, try to integrate the daily examen into your routine in order to recognize that God is with you, offering a compass to direct you down the paths he would like you to take.

Trustful Surrender to Divine Providence

Over three hundred years ago, the Jesuit spiritual writer St. Claude de la Colombière (1980) wrote *Trustful Surrender to Divine Providence*. In this short work, he outlined the "secret to peace and happiness," pointing to God's infinite wisdom, love, presence, and power to argue that surrendering to his will yields lasting results. In other words, because God is perfect, he knows what is best for his creation. Therefore, by submitting to God, Christians are able to find true contentment, given that God has the best possible plan, even in the midst of suffering (St. Claude de la Colombière, 1980).

In your daily struggles with uncertainty, doubt, worry, and anxiety, the "secret to peace and happiness" may involve practicing the ability to let go—trusting that God knows what is best for you, even as you look out into an uncertain, unknown future. During instances of ambiguity and uncertainty, you may find that St. Claude de la Colombière's spiritual wisdom can help you to recognize that God is all-knowing, all-loving, and all-powerful, providing for you as a caring, responsive father. What follows, therefore, is St. Claude de la Colombière's (1980) three-step process for yielding to God's loving, protective care, letting go of worry because of an increased certainty that he will provide.

Exercise: "Conformity to Divine Providence"

In *Trustful Surrender to Divine Providence*, St. Claude de la Colombière (1980)[1] presented a three-step strategy to surrender to God's providence on a daily basis. After reading about these three steps, noted below, see if you can find the time each day to move through his recommendations, placing your faith, hope, and love in God's sovereign, benevolent care on a daily basis. In fact, if you can, try to integrate this three-step process into your morning, midday, and evening rituals. After each time you practice, see if you can briefly reflect on the experience in a journal exercise, noted below.

1. "First make an act of faith in God's Providence. Meditate well on the truth that God's continual care extends not only to all things in general but to each particular thing, and especially to ourselves, our souls and bodies, and everything that concerns us. Nothing escapes His loving watchfulness—our work, our daily needs, our health as well as our infirmities, our life and our death, even the smallest hair on our head which cannot fall without His permission."

2. "After this act of faith, make an act of hope. Excite in yourself a firm trust that God will provide for all you need, will direct and protect you with more than a father's love and vigilance, and guide you in such a way that, whatever happens, if you submit to Him everything will turn out for your happiness and advantage, even the things that may seem quite the opposite."

3. "To these two an act of charity should be added. Show your deep love and attachment to Divine Providence as a child shows for its mother by taking refuge in her arms. Say how highly you esteem all His intentions, however hidden they may be, in the knowledge that they spring from an infinite wisdom which cannot make a mistake and supreme goodness which can wish only the perfection of His creatures. Determine that this feeling will have a practical result in making you ready to speak out in defense of Providence whenever you hear it denied or criticized."

Day of the Week	Practiced Three-Step Process of Surrender?	Experience of Uncertainty, Doubt, Worry, and Anxiety After the Exercise	Experience of God's Active, Loving Presence After the Exercise
Monday	Yes/No		
Tuesday	Yes/No		
Wednesday	Yes/No		
Thursday	Yes/No		
Friday	Yes/No		
Saturday	Yes/No		
Sunday	Yes/No		

EXERCISE: HOMEWORK FOR THE WEEK

1. Practice the above 20-minute "prayer of the senses" exercise at least once per day for the entire week. Document these experiences in the space provided above.

2. Journal for at least 10 minutes per day about the "prayer of the senses" exercise (in the space provided above), focusing on what the experience was like and any potential barriers (e.g., thoughts, feelings, sensations) to focusing on Jesus' teaching on worry via your senses.

3. At least three times per day, try to surrender to God's presence through St. Claude de la Colombière's (1980) "exercise of conformity to divine providence." Briefly reflect on these daily experiences in the space provided above.

Finding God in the Midst of Uncertainty: Perspectives from Erin, Ryan, and Lisa

In the third week of the program, Erin was really struggling with uncertainty and worry, recalling the pain she felt in childhood as her sense of stability was taken away. After her parents' divorce, her number one priority was to anticipate future disasters, predicting what might happen next as a way to ensure her safety. Yet, because life is unpredictable, she struggled in both her work life and social interactions.

When she began to look for God's active, loving presence in her daily experiences, she initially struggled to "find him." Given that she had learned to manage life on her own, which was (from her perspective) the safest strategy, noticing God's loving attentiveness was especially challenging. Yet, through the "prayer of the senses" exercise, she was able to embed herself in Jesus' sermon on worry, feeling her way into the experience in order to spend time with him. For Erin, this was an especially powerful experience, given that she felt God's presence in these instances. As she used her senses to interact with Jesus in his Sermon on the Mount, she found that talking to him was just what she needed.

After prayerfully considering the question she would ask him during her alone time with her Lord and Savior, she decided to ask Jesus why he was absent during her parents' divorce. As the question left her mouth, she noticed tears were rolling down her cheeks, and she felt a deep sense of sadness, along with the anxiety that was all too familiar. Waiting for a reply, she observed that Jesus had a look of concern on his face, responding in a simple manner, "I'm always with you."

Listening intently to his reply, Erin immediately recognized that she had assumed he was distant and cold. Yet, she began to reflect on her life, noticing that God might have been with her all along. Although this was too big of a revelation to fully absorb in one sitting, she found that practicing the "prayer of the senses" on a daily basis allowed her to continue to talk with Jesus on the breezy hillside, learning to surrender to God's providential care as Jesus powerfully declared that she need not worry.

For Ryan, cultivating a deeper awareness of God's presence in the third week of the program was also a challenge. Because he was utterly shocked when his girlfriend broke up with him, he found it very difficult to recognize that God was near, intervening in each passing moment. Given that he assumed God was either absent or punishing him for something he had done, Ryan approached the third week of the program with a sense of dread.

As he began to practice the "daily examen," he noticed that his view of God began to change, resembling the way in which he trusted God in childhood. As he reflected on each day, he was able to recognize God's active, loving presence, even when he was feeling anxious and uncertain. During moments of anxiety and isolation, he increasingly felt that God was ministering to him, with his anxiety serving as a signal that let him know he needed to surrender his cares to God. He also began to trust that God would see him through the ambiguity he was facing.

Although Ryan was still in pain from the breakup, he started to recognize that God was all-knowing, all-loving, and all-powerful. This unique combination of attributes, from Ryan's perspective, meant that God might know what is best for his life, even as he doubted God's providential care during the breakup. In other words, although Ryan most certainly did not have it all figured out, he began to move in the direction of trusting God, given that God was present, even when Ryan was hurting due to the loss. Rather than "spending the rest of his life alone," Ryan realized that God was with him, loving him and providing him with a sense of hope for the future.

With Lisa, the third week of the program brought on additional feelings of uncertainty and anxiety, given that she knew she would be asked to work on "finding God in all things"—quite a foreign concept. In Lisa's experiences, she learned that she was on her own, whether in childhood or after the tragic death of her husband. Over time, she concluded that, if God actually existed, he was distant and impersonal in that he seemed to allow the world to run without his active participation.

Yet, as Lisa started to practice St. Claude de la Colombière's (1980) three-step process for surrendering to God's providence, she experienced a deep sense of trust in God that she had not experienced before. Beginning with "faith," she worked on recognizing that "nothing escapes his loving watchfulness." As she reflected on this notion of trusting in God's active, loving care, she recognized that God was walking beside her during her most painful moments in life. Although he did not take her pain away, he helped her to endure and overcome, guiding her through these instances of immense suffering.

In addition, she started placing her hope in God, looking out into the future and seeing that God was illuminating her paths. Rather than viewing herself as all alone, reminiscent of her childhood years, she was determined to yield to God's omniscience, recognizing that his love and guidance were going to carve out a unique trajectory. In fact, God was walking by her side in both the immediate and distant future. In this future, she observed that God was helping her to find contentment and fulfillment, even in the midst of pain.

Finally, Lisa vowed to worship God, expressing a deep sense of loving awe for his ways. Instead of doubting that he had her best interests in mind, she decided to view him as a loving father who was protecting her and carrying her during low points, with his active presence extending out into the future. Although God's "intentions" may have been "hidden," she promised herself she would continue to love God, trusting that he would provide from moment to moment even though she struggled to believe in this reality as a child.

For Erin, Ryan, and Lisa, recognizing that God was active and present was not an easy task. Yet, because God is all-knowing, all-loving, and all-powerful, they began to notice that he was intervening from moment to moment, rather than waiting around in some sort of distant, far removed heaven. In moments of uncertainty, doubt, worry, and anxiety, each of them (in their own way) were able to begin the lifelong process of recognizing that God was with them in their pain, helping them with the ambiguities they were facing. Although they did not know what was ahead, the "prayer of the senses," "prayer of examen," and "exercise of conformity to divine providence" helped them to trust in God, rather than using "approach" or "avoidance" strategies to create a seemingly certain future, which only God knows.

CONCLUSION

In the third week, you were able to learn more about Ignatian spirituality, including its emphasis on "finding God in all things." Rather than viewing God as a distant, apathetic deity, the Jesuit tradition emphasizes that God loves you, cares for you, and is active and present, even in the midst of psychological pain. Applied to uncertainty, worry, and anxiety, God is with you when you do not know what lies ahead, helping to illuminate your paths and provide for you.

Through the "prayer of the senses," "prayer of examen," and "exercise of conformity to divine providence," our hope is that you are continuing to let go of your pursuit of certainty, recognizing that worrying cannot "add a single hour to your life" (Matthew 6:27). Instead, because God is all-knowing, all-loving, and all-powerful, he has your best intentions in mind, helping you to move through the storms of life with an attitude of hope and endurance. Along the way, God is attending to your needs, revealing himself to you as you struggle with worry and anxiety.

In the next chapter, you will begin to explore another form of prayer, drawing from the *apophatic* tradition. With the Jesus Prayer, which has roots in early desert spirituality, you will be calling out to Jesus, asking for his mercy and compassion when you are struggling with uncertainty, doubt, worry, and anxiety. As you reach out to him, you will be working on keeping him at the forefront of your day, praying over and over again to rest in his loving arms.

NOTE

1   The following three steps are quoted directly from St. Claude de la Colombière (1980, pp. 122–123).

REFERENCES

Fink, P. (2001). Finding God in All Things: Jesuit Spirituality. *Liturgical Ministry, 10*, 208–210.

Foster, R. (2011). *Sanctuary of the Soul: Journey into Meditative Prayer*. Downers Grove, IL: InterVarsity Press.

Hansen, G. (2012). *Kneeling with Giants: Learning to Pray with History's Best Teachers*. Downers Grove, IL: InterVarsity Press.

Ignatian Spirituality. (n.d.). *The Daily Examen*. Retrieved March 3, 2016 from www.ignatianspirituality.com

Ignatian Spirituality. (n.d.). *What Are the Spiritual Exercises?* Retrieved April 1, 2016 from www.ignatianspirituality.com

Jackson, C. (n.d.). *Ignatian Spirituality*. Washington, DC: Jesuit Conference.

St. Claude de la Colombière. (1980). *Trustful Surrender to Divine Providence: The Secret of Peace and Happiness*. Charlotte, NC: Tan Books.

Warner, L. (2010). *Journey with Jesus: Discovering the Spiritual Exercises of Saint Ignatius*. Downers Grove, IL: InterVarsity Press.

Week 4

THE JESUS PRAYER

Introduction

In the fourth week of the program, you will learn more about the history of the Jesus Prayer, "Lord Jesus Christ, Son of God, have mercy on me, a sinner," which likely dates back to the second half of the first millennium. With this prayer, which has roots in both the writings of the early desert Christians and the Greek Orthodox Church, you will practice praying continuously, reminiscent of several passages in scripture. Moreover, consistent with several instances of individuals crying out to Jesus for mercy in the gospels, you will recite this powerful prayer as a way to yield to God's active, loving presence, remembering his grace, mercy, and compassion throughout your day.

Beyond learning about the Jesus Prayer, you will be able to apply the prayer to your struggles with uncertainty, worry, and anxiety, reciting this 12-word prayer both formally and informally throughout your day. Our hope is that the prayer will help you to cultivate a deeper trust in God, especially when you are anxious about what the future will hold, letting go of worry because Jesus is ministering to you and offering you his loving mercy from moment to moment. Along the way, you will be able to practice the Jesus Prayer in a quiet environment, sitting with Jesus as you ask him to respond to your pain with a compassionate, empathic understanding. Because he is with you, we believe the Jesus Prayer can serve as a reminder that Jesus is a trustworthy travel companion on the rugged trails of life.

A Brief History of the Jesus Prayer

Within the gospels, Jesus offered himself as *the* way for his followers to reconcile with God (John 14:6), teaching that his disciples were to petition God in his name (John 16:23–24). Within the gospel of John, these types of teachings illuminate the power of Jesus' name. As a twenty-first-century example, many Christians casually end prayers with "in Jesus' name," without recognizing the importance of this concluding remark. Yet, from a biblical perspective, Jesus' name is especially important in the spiritual life of Christians, including those who are struggling within contemporary society.

In addition to focusing on Jesus' name, there are several instances in the gospels that involve someone asking Jesus for mercy. For example, in Matthew 15, the gospel writer told the story of a Canaanite who powerfully exclaimed, "Lord, Son of David, have mercy on me!" In this instance, she was asking for Jesus' compassion and healing, given that her child was "suffering terribly." Although Jesus initially responded by stating that he was born to save "the lost sheep of Israel," the woman persisted, faithfully asking again for Jesus to respond to her daughter's pain. Because of her faith, Jesus answered her plea, healing her suffering child.

Along with other instances in the gospels, this chapter in Matthew's depiction of Jesus' life and ministry highlights the importance of faith in following Jesus, crying out to him during moments of suffering. Although Jesus does not always heal our wounds, asking him for a compassionate, merciful reply can strengthen our ability to endure by finding hope in his presence. A poignant example is Jesus' experience with Lazarus (John 11). Jesus heard about the illness of his friend Lazarus when Lazarus' sisters sent the news to Jesus. Jesus waited for two days before traveling to Lazarus so that "[t]his sickness will not end in death. No, it is for God's glory so that God's Son may be glorified through it" (John 11:4). After two days, Jesus traveled to Lazarus' home, discovering that Lazarus had died. The text is plain at this point: "Jesus wept" (John 11:35). The point is, through suffering and death on the cross, Jesus is able to support and understand our human suffering with divine compassion. Therefore, Jesus' name (in and of itself), along with the ability to reach for him during painful experiences, is especially important in the Christian life.

To offer one more biblical illustration of the roots of the Jesus Prayer, Paul instructed the Thessalonians to "rejoice always, pray continually, give thanks in all circumstances; for this is God's will for you in Christ Jesus" (1 Thessalonians 5:16–18). Here, we see that Paul was helping his audience to consistently pray, thanking God in the midst of all kinds of trials. Based on this New Testament teaching, the Jesus Prayer can help you to cry out to God in the midst of pain, cultivating a deeper faith in him from moment to moment as you ask for him to respond to you with mercy and compassion. Because of the power of his name, along with Jesus' empathy, repeating the Jesus Prayer throughout your day can help you to constantly remember his promises, along with his desire to pursue you and minister to your needs.

Over time, these biblical teachings began to resonate deeply with early Christians, including Origen, who lived in the second and third century. Interestingly, Origen wrote the following in reference to Jesus' name:

> The name of Jesus can still remove distractions from the minds of men, and expel demons, and also take away diseases; and produce a marvelous meekness of spirit and complete change of character, and a humanity, and goodness, and gentleness in those individuals who do not feign themselves to be Christians. (quoted in Chumley, 2011, p. 89)

In addition to Origen, desert monks began to recite brief prayers as a way to focus on God throughout their day, often memorizing and reciting the Psalms while they endured boredom and other distractions in solitude. Eventually, several monastic writings recommended repeating Jesus' name, typically in unison with the in-breath and out-breath (Laird, 2006).

In contemporary times, the Greek Orthodox Church is a staunch advocate for the regular use of the Jesus Prayer for spiritual health. Within the pages of the *Philokalia*, a collection of contemplative writings that span several centuries, reciting the Jesus Prayer is consistently taught in order to achieve a state of calmness and stillness, referred to as *hesychia*.

EASTERN ORTHODOX SPIRITUALITY AND THE JESUS PRAYER

Within the Orthodox Church, the Jesus Prayer is recited in order to maintain a sense of calm stillness (the Greek word *hesychia*). In this tranquil, quiet state, the mind is focused on the name of Jesus, with the words of the prayer eventually reciting themselves in the practitioner's heart.

Commonly referred to as the "Prayer of the Heart," some of the more common characteristics of stillness are as follows (adapted from Wong, 2010):

- Inner peace and quiet within the depths of the heart.
- Transcending distracting thoughts within the heart.
- Spending time with God in solitude.
- Focusing on God's active, loving presence.
- Turning inward in order to find God dwelling within the heart.

In fact, below are some specific teachings from the *Philokalia* on the Jesus Prayer in order to give you a sense of the benefits (from an Eastern Orthodox perspective):

Truly blessed is the man whose mind and heart are as closely attached to the Jesus Prayer and to the cease-less invocation of his name as air to the body or flames to the wax. The sun rising over the earth creates the daylight; and the venerable and holy name of the Lord Jesus, shining continually in the mind, gives birth to countless intellections as radiant as the sun. (St. Hesychios the Priest quoted in Smith, 2006, p. 111)

Smoke from wood kindling a fire troubles the eyes; but then the fire gives them light and gladdens them. Similarly, unceasing attentiveness is irksome; but when, invoked in prayer, Jesus draws near, he illumines the heart; for remembrance of him confers on us spiritual enlightenment and the highest of all blessings. (St. Pilotheos of Sinai quoted in Smith, 2006, p. 115)

THE MAIN INGREDIENTS OF THE JESUS PRAYER

As noted above, the main elements of the Jesus Prayer involve repeating the prayer with the in-breath and out-breath, along with reaching out to God, asking Jesus for compassion and mercy (Wong, 2010). In fact, breaking down the prayer into smaller parts can be helpful in your efforts to better understand its strengths (adapted from Talbot, 2013):

- Lord: To think of Jesus as "Lord" means that he is sovereign, serving as our master and guide for daily living. With this understanding in mind, he is in control, orchestrating life's events. Therefore, rather than attempting to attain our own certainty through worrying and employing "approach" and "avoidance" strategies, Christians are to yield to his authority, bowing to him on the throne.
- Jesus Christ: Since Jesus is Christians' path to salvation, dying on a wooden cross for the sins of humankind, he offers himself to us in an altruistic, loving manner. As a result, in the midst of uncertainty, doubt, worry, and anxiety, he is responsive, consistent with the incarnation—God became a human being because he loves his creation, entering into human history in order to respond to a fallen and broken world.
- Son of God: By focusing on these words of the Jesus Prayer, Christians are remembering that Jesus is part of the Trinity—Father, Son, and Holy Spirit—which is one of the greatest mysteries of the Christian faith. Rather than trying to fully comprehend this awe-inspiring mystery, we can simply recognize that God is relational, creating us in his image to be in relationship with him.
- Have Mercy on Me: With this request for Jesus' mercy, Christians are asking for Jesus to compassionately respond to our fragile, vulnerable state, reaching out to Jesus as a way to connect to him in our moment of pain. Reminiscent of the gospel accounts of people

asking Jesus for mercy, we are asking for Jesus to be present, understanding our predicament as we struggle with the reality of the human condition.

- A Sinner: With this phrase, we are acknowledging that we fall short, struggling to create a life worth living without God's active, loving presence. Because Jesus is Lord, we can cry out to him for his compassionate, merciful reply, recognizing when we have drifted away with our own unilateral efforts to achieve certainty, predictability, and safety. As we conclude the Jesus Prayer, we are confessing to Jesus that we need him, yielding to him as *the* source of life.

Another important aspect of the Jesus Prayer is the use of breathing when reciting the prayer (Talbot, 2013). The Hebrew (*ruach*) and Greek (*pneuma*) words for spirit also mean breath and wind (Talbot, 2013), quite an interesting notion when considering the role of breathing in contemplative practice. As you may recall in Genesis (2:7), God breathed into Adam the "breath of life." In combining the Jesus Prayer with one's breathing, we re-experience the prayer moment by moment—with each breath. Talbot (2013) reminds us: "Breathing in fills us up, and breathing out empties us. Breathing in causes us to hold on, and breathing out causes us to let go" (p. 17). By pairing this prayer with breath, we hold onto Jesus as Lord, and we let go to experience forgiveness and salvation.

EXERCISE: REFLECTING ON THE JESUS PRAYER

In the space that follows, see if you can reflect on what each part of the Jesus Prayer means to you in your current relationship with God (in positive terms). In other words, as you learn about this famous prayer, try to jot down some of your own initial reactions, taking into consideration your current struggles with uncertainty, doubt, worry, and anxiety.

- Lord:

  _____

- Jesus Christ:

  _____

- Son of God:

  _____

- Have Mercy on Me:

  _____

- A Sinner:

  _____

POSSIBLE BENEFITS OF THE JESUS PRAYER: A HOLISTIC UNDERSTANDING

Although the list below is by no means exhaustive, we believe there are several overlapping spiritual and psychological benefits to the Jesus Prayer:

- The prayer can help you to focus your mind on God, including his promise of grace and acceptance, pivoting away from a preoccupation with uncertainty.

- The prayer can help you to redirect your worrying mind towards the powerful name of Jesus, especially when you are caught up in using worry as a way to "fill in the blanks" apart from God.
- The prayer can help you to move towards *hesychia*, cultivating a deeper stillness and inner silence, rather than employing worry to achieve a pseudo-certain state. By way of this stillness and silence in the present moment, we cultivate a deeper intimacy with God in daily living (Tan & Gregg, 1997).
- The prayer can help you to develop the ability to surrender to God's active, loving presence, emphasizing God's mercy as you cry out to him during instances of worry and doubt.
- The prayer can help you to maintain an awareness of your need for God's sustenance for survival, confessing that you have wandered away and that you need him to minister to your needs, especially when you are hurting due to ambiguity and uncertainty.
- The prayer can help you to recognize that you are not alone in an uncertain, unpredictable world; instead, you are calling out to a God who is all-knowing, all-loving, and all-powerful. In this prayer, we are relying on God's mercy, as expressed in Jesus' sacrifice.
- The prayer can help you to pray throughout the day in order to deepen your relationship with God, acknowledging that Jesus is the Lord of your life. This happens especially when connecting the prayer to one's breath.
- The prayer can help you to stay rooted in the present moment, walking with Jesus throughout your day, rather than anticipating some sort of doomsday scenario unfolding in a yet-to-be-determined future. It facilitates our ability to pray continually (1 Thessalonians 5:17).

EXERCISE: IDENTIFYING YOUR OWN PERCEIVED BENEFITS OF THE JESUS PRAYER

See if you can come up with some of your own anticipated benefits of the Jesus Prayer. In other words, based on the above ingredients, how might the prayer help you in your own struggles with worry, doubt, uncertainty, and anxiety?

1. _____

_____

2. _____

_____

3. _____

_____

4. _____

_____

5. _____

_____

Instructions for the Jesus Prayer

With the Jesus Prayer, you will be gently reciting the following words: "Lord Jesus Christ, Son of God, have mercy on me, a sinner." Although there are several forms of the prayer, including various condensed versions, we believe that the full version has all of the ingredients to address your uncertainty, worry, and anxiety. To be sure, in this practice, you are calling out to Jesus as both your Lord and the Son of God, drawing from the Christian belief that Jesus is part of the Trinity—Father, Son, and Holy Spirit. What is more, you are asking Jesus to have compassion and empathy (Talbot, 2013) for you as you struggle with difficult inner experiences, confessing that you have lost your way and need to surrender to him so that he can help you in your time of need.

The Jesus Prayer can be practiced both formally—usually reciting the prayer around 100 times or spending about 20 to 30 minutes with the prayer, slowly saying it over and over again—and informally throughout your day. This is why breathing is so important in using this prayer. Our breath is a reminder of a moment-by-moment need for God's mercy. Many practitioners recognize that the prayer begins to recite itself, given that you are saying it repeatedly. This is consistent with St. Theophan the Recluse: "At first this saving prayer is usually a matter of strenuous effort and hard work. But if one concentrates on it with zeal it will begin to flow of its own accord, like a brook that murmurs in the heart" (quoted in Johnston, 1997, p. 94).

In turn, practitioners begin to "pray continuously," consistent with the previously noted instructions from the New Testament. As you say the prayer gently and consistently, you are learning to embed it in your heart, rather than employing the prayer merely as a cognitive endeavor. In other words, you are imagining that the words are buried deep within your heart, instead of in your head.

Consistent with Talbot (2013), we recommend aligning the prayer with your natural breathing patterns, saying "Lord Jesus Christ, Son of God" as you breathe in, and "have mercy on me, a sinner" as you breathe out. If you can, try to do this naturally, rather than forcing the breath in any way. Given that you are trying to let the words repeat themselves, you do not want to force them, or somehow become preoccupied with your breathing. Because your breathing occurs naturally, see if you can just insert the words into the natural rhythm of your breath, recognizing that God is giving you your breathing as a gift. He is sustaining you and giving you life.

The three main steps of the Jesus Prayer are as follows (adapted from Brianchaninov, 2013):

- Gently start to say the Jesus Prayer out loud, focusing on the actual meaning and importance of the words: "Lord Jesus Christ, Son of God, have mercy on me, a sinner."
- Next, you will begin to notice that your mind is busy and distracting you with a stream of thoughts, which is perfectly normal and should not derail the practice. When you notice that your mind has drifted towards a thought other than the words of the Jesus Prayer, compassionately pivot back towards the prayer, focusing exclusively on Jesus' presence.
- Over time, you will begin to recite the prayer within your heart, which is the core of who you are and where God is ministering to you, deep within the foundation of your soul. In this third and final step, Jesus is doing all of the work, given that the prayer is likely reciting itself and you are letting go of your own efforts; instead, God's grace and mercy are leading the way. In this last step, you may find that your inner world is silent, calm, and still—*hesychia*—since you are simply allowing God to work within, without striving to do anything on your part. By now, the words of the prayer are beginning to penetrate your inner being, resulting in the ability to let go of your own efforts.

THE JESUS PRAYER, STILLNESS, AND UNCERTAINTY, WORRY, AND ANXIETY

In our view, over time, the prayer can begin to stir within your inner being, with Jesus residing at the center of your existence. If you can stay consistent with the prayer, both formally and informally, we believe that these powerful words can help you with your uncertainty, doubt, and worry for a few overlapping reasons that are noted below:

- Focusing on the Jesus Prayer can help you to cultivate sustained attention, attentively pivoting towards Jesus' presence in each moment; this is in contrast to fortune-telling because you are uncertain and worried about what tomorrow will bring. Remember that our very breath is a gift from God, and we are relying on God to help us breathe moment by moment.
- By letting the actual words of the prayer penetrate your heart, you are developing an attitude of surrender, fortifying your relationship with Jesus because he is carving out your paths and walking with you along the roads of life.
- Along the way, you are asking Jesus to have compassion for you, empathizing with your experience; therefore, you are not on your own when handling the stressors of tomorrow. As you stay focused on Jesus, you are deepening your intimacy with him, trusting that he is all-knowing, all-loving, and all-powerful. This reality means you can let go of your own unilateral attempts to gain control and certainty.
- Given that worry is about achieving a state of certainty, with anxiety pointing to a seemingly dangerous, unstable future, the Jesus Prayer is a way to shift your focus to what matters most—God's sovereign, benevolent presence. In other words, relying on Christ's mercy to us—sinners. Because he is actively intervening in your life, you can "transfer the reins to him," reminiscent of a child who is safely tucked in bed, knowing that his mother and father are in the room next door. Certainly, the child's parents are ready to respond to his needs should danger arise in the middle of the night.
- Above all else, reciting the words of the Jesus Prayer, which will eventually begin to reside in your heart, can help the choppy waves of the inner world to settle, reminiscent of Jesus calming the storm as his disciples panicked in the boat on the lake. Because Jesus was in control, he calmly responded, "[rebuking] the winds and waves" (Matthew 8:23–27).

EXERCISE: 20-MINUTE JESUS PRAYER MEDITATION

Now that you have had the opportunity to learn more about the Jesus Prayer, we would like for you to begin to practice (adapted from Talbot, 2013). If possible, try to find a comfortable place to settle in, sitting up straight with your feet gently resting on the floor. If you can, try to maintain a normal, natural rhythm for your breathing patterns, given that you will be aligning the in-breath with the first half of the prayer, and the out-breath with the second half. When you are ready, close your eyes and begin to recite the prayer. You can also follow along with the 20-minute audio file that has been provided (Track 3 at https://www.routledge.com/Contemplative-Prayer-for-Christians-with-Chronic-Worry-An-Eight-Week-Program/Knabb-Frederick/p/book/9781138690943 under the eResource tab).

- Please begin by closing your eyes, settling into your chair. Say a brief prayer, asking Jesus to be with you during this time, requesting his guidance in order to surrender to him as the Lord of your life. You can also ask him to help you with your uncertainty and worry, letting go of the tendency to unilaterally attempt to create a certain future. You are asking him to guide your paths, even when you are not sure where they will lead.

- Next, begin to notice your breathing, recognizing that God is giving you your breathing as a gift. He is giving you life, which is captured in your breathing. What an amazing gift that God has provided, creating you to breathe on your own, without needing to do anything to force your breathing in any way. As you notice your in-breath and out-breath, begin to whisper the powerful words of the Jesus Prayer out loud, "Lord Jesus Christ, Son of God" with the in-breath, and "have mercy on me, a sinner" with the out-breath. If you can, try to do this gently and slowly, aligning the words naturally with the organic flow of your breath, which God is controlling.

- At a certain point, you will notice that you are distracted by a range of thoughts, some of which may revolve around uncertainty, doubt, and worry. As you notice these thoughts, just acknowledge that your mind has shifted, pivoting back to the prayer with love and compassion. Remember, try not to be critical or judgmental towards your inner distractions; instead, continue to shift back to Jesus' mercy, empathy, and compassion, recognizing that he is loving you and ministering to your needs in this very moment.

- Again and again, recite the prayer, beginning to say the words in your heart, rather than out loud. You may even want to imagine that they are located in your heart, instead of focusing on "thinking" them in your head. Since Jesus lives in your innermost being, he is dwelling in your heart, offering you mercy and grace from moment to moment as he lifts you up, sustains you, and responds to your pain.

- In your gentle efforts to recite the prayer, really sink into the actual words, recognizing that Jesus is the Lord of your life—he is in control. Because of this, you can let go of your own efforts to attain certainty, using worry to predict the future and "problem solve" about what comes next.

- Repeat the words "Lord Jesus Christ, Son of God, have mercy on me, a sinner," gently saying them in your heart as you sink deeper and deeper into an awareness of God's active, loving presence. In this very moment, Jesus understands you and is with you, loving you in the midst of your uncertainty and worry.

- Continue to return to the prayer when your attention has drifted, reciting the words with constancy and devotion to your Lord and Savior, recognizing that he is powerful and actively, mercifully working within your inner world. He is even active when you are not aware of what he is doing. As this practice comes to a close, give Jesus thanks, worshipping him by trusting in his active presence. Recognize that he is your Lord and understands you (even when you are possibly confused about who you are and what your next steps will be in this unpredictable world).

Once you have finished the 20-minute meditation for the first time, try to document your experience. What was it like to recite the Jesus Prayer over and over again? What, if anything, got in the way of reciting the prayer? Were you able to successfully pivot back to the Jesus Prayer when you noticed you were worrying or feeling anxious? In linking the prayer with your breath, how did you experience holding onto "Lord Jesus Christ"? What did you experience in letting go of your breath on "Have mercy on me, a sinner"? What might it be like to recite the Jesus Prayer for the rest of your day, trusting that God is active and present as he loves you and sustains you with his mercy and compassion?

_____

_____

_____

_____

_____

_____

_____

EXERCISE: RECORDING YOUR DAILY EFFORTS FOR THE JESUS PRAYER

In the space that follows, see if you can briefly document your daily experience of the Jesus Prayer (beyond what you have documented in the space above).

Day of the Week	Length of Time Practiced (Minutes)	Experience of Uncertainty, Doubt, Worry, and Anxiety Before and After the Practice	Experience of God's Active, Loving Presence Before and After the Practice	Inner Barriers to the Jesus Prayer (Thoughts, Feelings, and Sensations)	Outer Barriers to the Jesus Prayer (Distractions in the Environment)
Monday					
Tuesday					
Wednesday					
Thursday					
Friday					
Saturday					
Sunday					

THE JESUS PRAYER

EXERCISE: JOURNALING ABOUT YOUR EXPERIENCE OF THE JESUS PRAYER

In the space below, try to journal about your experience of the Jesus Prayer on a daily basis (beyond what you have documented in the space above). You may wish to explore your relationship with God, as well as your inner experience of uncertainty, doubt, worry, and anxiety before and after the practice.

Monday

Tuesday

Wednesday

Thursday

Friday

THE JESUS PRAYER

Saturday

_____

Sunday

_____

ADDITIONAL REFLECTIONS ON MERCY

From our vantage point, the most important part of the Jesus Prayer involves your willingness to cry out to Jesus for mercy, acknowledging that you are giving him total control of your life. In fact, the various passages in the gospels that mention individuals asking Jesus for mercy seem to illuminate the importance of Jesus' help in a critical time of need (Mathewes-Green, 2011). When this act of surrender is repeated throughout your day, we believe you will be in a better position to deal with uncertainty, given that you are practicing trusting in Jesus to illuminate your paths. To ask for mercy, certainly, involves taking a courageous step in a different direction, given that you may have struggled with letting go of control thus far in your life.

Although Jesus continuously offers us mercy even when we do not ask for it (Mathewes-Green, 2011), we firmly believe that petitioning Jesus for mercy can help you to cultivate a deeper willingness to let go of your own efforts to generate a certain future, divorced from him. Interestingly, "mercy" in Greek (*eleos*) can mean olive oil, pointing to the role that mercy plays in healing wounds and comforting the afflicted individual as he or she longs to be nursed back to health (Coniaris, 1998). The meaning of *eleos* points to the fact that we have already experienced God's mercy in the past. However, this mercy continues from that point forward. In other words, we once experienced God's mercy, and this mercy continues from that point throughout eternity. For Talbot (2013), mercy captures Jesus' compassionate empathy, elucidating his firm desire to understand us and respond to our cry for help.

Remember the Apostle Paul's powerful experience, documented in his second letter to the Corinthians:

> I was given a thorn in my flesh, a messenger of Satan, to torment me. Three times I pleaded with the Lord to take it away from me. But he said to me, "My grace is sufficient for you, for my power is made perfect in weakness." Therefore I will boast all the more gladly about my weaknesses, so that Christ's power may rest on me. That is why, for Christ's sake, I delight in weaknesses, in insults, in hardships, in persecutions, in difficulties. For when I am weak, then I am strong. (2 Corinthians 12:7–10)

Paul's experience reminds us that Jesus' mercy and grace are enough—for Paul and for us. We must rely on God's mercy. As Jesus teaches us (see Matthew 6), praying for our daily needs is something we are called to do. In the Jesus Prayer, we are reminded not only of our need for daily bread, but that we are in need of God's moment-by-moment breath.

Overall, crying out to God for mercy can help us to run towards God's outstretched arms, reminiscent of the story of the lost son, who had wandered away (Luke 15:11–32). In this story, the son eventually realized he had drifted too far from home, struggling to make ends meet on his own. Therefore, he turned around, walking back after a long period of time with a sense of shame and hurt. Yet, his father was waiting for him, even running to his son when he noticed his son coming back.

Similarly, the Jesus Prayer can help you to receive God's soothing, comforting, and compassionate mercy, falling into his outstretched arms during moments of uncertainty, worry, and anxiety. Although you may have tried on your own to make ends meet, striving for unilateral certainty in a hostile world, God is waiting for you with his loving arms. He is ready to love you and care for you with his providence guiding the way. Because God is all-knowing, all-loving, and all-powerful, returning over and over again to his outstretched arms—via the Jesus Prayer—can be helpful in your efforts to ameliorate chronic worry and anxiety.

EXERCISE: HOMEWORK FOR THE WEEK

1. Practice the above 20-minute Jesus Prayer exercise at least once per day for the entire week. Document these experiences in the space provided above.
2. Journal for at least 10 minutes per day about the Jesus Prayer exercise (in the space provided above), focusing on what the experience was like and any potential barriers (e.g., thoughts, feelings, sensations).
3. Try to recite the Jesus Prayer throughout your day, beyond the formal practice, in order to "pray continually" (1 Thessalonians 5:16–18).

Asking Jesus for Compassion and Mercy: Perspectives from Erin, Ryan, and Lisa

As Erin transitioned into the fourth week of the program, she felt as though she was making some progress, especially when embedding herself in Jesus' Sermon on the Mount through the "prayer of the senses." Yet, she still struggled to accept an uncertain future, frequently wandering away from Jesus when she did not know what would happen next in her life. Consistent with her experience of her parents' divorce, she was deathly afraid of being "blindsided" by another unexpected occurrence, given that she originally concluded that her parents' divorce was her fault. Although as an adult she knew that it was not her fault, a small part of her still wondered, blaming herself and believing that she could have done something to change the outcome.

Because her father abruptly left in her childhood, in her adult years she experienced a significant wound, which would flare up from time to time when the days, weeks, and months ahead were cloudy and unclear. For Erin, an unknown future meant that there would be disaster ahead, which she believed she could not tolerate; therefore, she would frequently strive to compulsively manage her environment, to the point that she would feel drained and exhausted by the end of the week.

As she started to practice the Jesus Prayer, she noticed she was especially drawn to the "mercy" part, holding on to the word as a way to feel Jesus' presence. Although she did not feel supported or loved in her childhood years, she recognized that she could increasingly let go when reciting the prayer, allowing Jesus to minister to her and tend to her nagging injury from her vulnerable childhood. Seeing Jesus as a sort of physician, she looked forward to the moments she could repeat the prayer, recognizing that Jesus had his arms stretched wide open and was ready to embrace her and comfort her in her time of need.

Over the course of the week, she was able to pivot towards the prayer when she felt uncertain, worried, and anxious, slowly coming to the realization that Jesus was always with her and holding her as she struggled with ambiguity. Although she was unable to fully grasp what was around the corner, she found that she was increasingly able to let go, trusting that Jesus had her best intentions in mind because he is all-knowing, all-loving, and all-powerful.

In Ryan's view, the fourth week was much easier than the third. As he recited the Jesus Prayer, he found that he was increasingly confident in God's promises, recalling the safety he felt in childhood as he reached out to God to receive God's loving care. In fact, Ryan was especially drawn to the reference to "Lord," recognizing that he could trust Jesus to guide his paths from moment to moment.

Looking back on his college breakup, he began to recognize that God was carving out a new road for him and offering his providential care. Although Ryan still wondered why God would cause him so much pain, he was slowly learning to trust that, because Jesus was offering him compassion, empathy, and soothing comfort, he could let go of the tendency to use his thinking mind to "fill in the blanks" about the future. In other words, Ryan recognized that his worry was an attempt to gain certainty within his life; yet, because Jesus was God's Son, he needed to yield to Jesus' loving care by surrendering his need for control to God.

Instead of procrastinating about decisions, Ryan found that he was cultivating a deeper confidence in his relationship with Jesus, allowing Jesus to walk with him throughout his day through the repetition of the Jesus Prayer. Building on last week's insights, Ryan took another step forward, reaching for a God who was offering him "oil" to sooth the wound of a confusing breakup some time ago. Viewing Jesus as all-loving and all-powerful, to be sure, helped him to recognize that God had his best intentions in mind because God is love.

As Lisa transitioned to the fourth week of the program, she noticed she was especially longing for God to provide her with a sense of availability and comfort. Consistent with the prior week, she wanted to find peace in God's loving arms, given that she struggled in childhood with being able to lean on a caregiver in her loneliness and isolation. In fact, after her husband died, she was even more aware of this deep wound, which led to compulsive checking and a frequent desire to be reassured.

Still, as she began to recite the Jesus Prayer, she noticed that she found comfort in her ability to cry out to him in the midst of her pain, uncertainty, and doubt. Recognizing that he was with her as she recited the prayer, she slowly learned to allow the powerful words of the Jesus Prayer to take root deep within her heart. This led to an awareness that God was working and ministering to her needs. Although she continued to have anxiety throughout her day, she was able to quickly pivot towards the prayer, which offered her comfort and encouragement as she confessed to Jesus that she needed him more than anything else in the world. Because he was with her, offering her his love, presence, and power, she increasingly strived to surrender to his Lordship. She recognized that he was offering her understanding, compassion, and a freedom from her unilateral, worried attempts to travel down life's paths on her own.

CONCLUSION

In the fourth week, our hope is that you were able to begin the lifelong process of continuously praying throughout your day, calling out to Jesus, who can offer you love, support, comfort, and understanding during life's inevitable trials and hardships. Rather than striving to attain certainty on your own, we believe that the Jesus Prayer can help you to yield to Jesus' Lordship, recognizing that he has always been present to minister to your needs. He is even with you when the storms of life simply will not subside.

Although you may continue to experience uncertainty, worry, doubt, and anxiety, Jesus is walking by your side, responding to your calls for his loving, merciful arms to embrace you and comfort you. In addition to formally practicing the prayer, informal practice can help you to regularly cultivate an attitude of surrender, recognizing that Jesus is present, engaged, and excited about your life. He is willing to nurse your wounds with loving compassion. As the prayer begins to repeat itself, we believe that you will increasingly recognize that Jesus' presence is more than enough, given that the aches and pains of life may not fully go away. Yet, walking with him can help you to draw from his strength, recognizing that you were never designed to go it alone. As a light for your path, Jesus' name can help you to see more clearly, even when there are dangerous roads ahead.

In the next chapter, you will learn about centering prayer, which can help you to further draw from the *apophatic* tradition, recognizing that yielding to God's active, loving presence can help you in your time of need. Although you might not always "feel" God's presence, he is certainly working behind the scenes, providing you with key psychological and spiritual nutrients to endure whatever you are going through. As you consistently surrender to his providential care, we believe you will continue to improve in your ability to let go of a recurrent, compulsive striving for certainty. You may even begin to recognize that Jesus' yoke is easy and his burden is light (Matthew 11:30).

REFERENCES

Brianchaninov, I. (2013). *On the Prayer of Jesus*. Boston, MA: New Seeds Books.

Chumley, N. (2011). *Mysteries of the Jesus Prayer: Experiencing the Presence of God and a Pilgrimage to the Heart of an Ancient Spirituality*. New York: HarperCollins Publishers.

Coniaris, A. (1998). *Philokalia: The Bible of Orthodox Spirituality*. Minneapolis, MN: Light & Life Publishing Company.

Johnston, W. (1997). *The Inner Eye of Love: Mysticism and Religion*. New York: Fordham University Press.

Laird, M. (2006). *Into the Silent Land: A Guide to the Christian Practice of Contemplation*. New York: Oxford University Press.

Mathewes-Green, F. (2011). *Praying the Jesus Prayer*. Brewster, MA: Paraclete Press.

Smith, A. (2006). *Philokalia: The Easter Christian Spiritual Texts*. Woodstock, VT: SkyLight Paths Publishing.

Talbot, J. (2013). *The Jesus Prayer: A Cry for Mercy, a Path of Renewal*. Downers Grove, IL: InterVarsity Press.

Tan, S., & Gregg, D. (1997). *Disciplines of the Holy Spirit: How to Connect to the Spirit's Power and Presence*. Grand Rapids, MI: Zondervan.

Wong, J. (2010). The Jesus Prayer and Inner Stillness. *Religion East & West, 10*, 35–48.

WEEK 5

AN INTRODUCTION TO CENTERING PRAYER

INTRODUCTION

In the fifth week of the program, you will learn about the history and central ingredients of centering prayer, which has grown in popularity over the last several decades. With roots in the contemplative tradition, centering prayer is a contemporary version of a form of prayer presented in *The Cloud of Unknowing* (Bangley, 2006), helping Christians to sit with God in silence beyond thoughts, feelings, and sensations. Rather than using language to understand God, centering prayer is *apophatic*, allowing practitioners to yield to God's active, loving presence during formal practice without the distraction of words, thoughts, or images. Because of this, we believe centering prayer can help you during instances of uncertainty, worry, doubt, and anxiety, letting go of the need to manage and control the future on your own.

After exploring the roots and main ingredients of the practice, you will begin to experience this form of silent prayer, asking God to "work behind the scenes" to help you in your moments of need. Instead of actively working to "problem solve," you will be developing the habit of surrendering to God by trusting that he is healing your inner world, even when you do not "feel" his loving hand. Further, centering prayer allows us to acknowledge God's active presence for our good—both within our inner being and in the details of our life. As you spend time in solitude with God, our hope is that you will begin to recognize the various patterns of your mind, including the plethora of distracting thoughts that may be pulling you away from your ability to rest in him.

What is more, we all have the tendency to develop a false sense of self, which will be explored in detail within this week of the program. Unfortunately, when we attempt to obtain our value, safety, and status (Keating, 1997) from anything or anyone other than God, we are likely to discover that what we have reached for does not provide lasting, deeply satisfying results. On the other hand, through centering prayer, you may find you are able to begin moving in the direction of self-emptying, shedding the false self because of God's active, loving presence. Given that God is all-knowing, all-loving, and all-powerful, you can take off the proverbial armor that you have so tightly held onto over the years. In other words, you might be able to forgo your futile efforts to obtain certainty in "earthly things," instead of relying on God, the heavenly Father, to give you your daily bread (Matthew 6:11). In fact, you might frequently experience life as a battlefield that seems to require constant vigilance in the face of enemy invasions, surprise attacks, and so on.

Because centering prayer is foundational to our eight-week program, we will attempt to break down this form of contemplative practice into its basic parts, walking with you through this week in order to help you apply this simple form of prayer to your daily life. Along the way, you will likely experience a range of inner experiences, including distracting thoughts, painful feelings, and difficult sensations. Yet, we believe that this form of prayer can be especially relevant to your current predicament, aiding you in your efforts to find comfort in God's availability and strength.

A Short History of Centering Prayer

About four decades ago, several Trappist monks in the United States began to write about the main ingredients of centering prayer, inspired by the instructions presented in *The Cloud of Unknowing* (Keating, 1997). Interestingly, within the last 50 years or so, there has been renewed interest in Eastern forms of meditation, with some devout Christians even drawn towards these types of meditative practices; yet, within the Christian faith, there is also a rich heritage, with many Christians unaware of Christ-centered meditative practices within the contemplative literature (Pennington & Keating, 2007).

With centering prayer, practitioners are advised to say a brief prayer to God, asking for him to be active within their inner world during formal practice (Pennington, 1999). In turn, a prayer word is selected (typically a short word, consisting of one or two syllables), which merely serves as a symbolic gesture, with practitioners reciting the word to surrender to God's active, loving presence (Pennington, 1999). This idea of surrender involves consenting to accept whatever experiences God brings to our attention in the process. Additionally, we consent and acknowledge that God has our best interests at heart. God is for us, and God is with us even when it is difficult to experience him. Finally, whenever there is a distracting thought, feeling, or sensation that arises, practitioners are encouraged to compassionately and gently return their attention to the pre-selected prayer word, which they repeat again and again in an effort to yield to God's sovereignty over their inner world (Pennington, 1999).

During this formal prayer time, practitioners usually close their eyes, sitting up in a comfortable chair. Of course, the most important part of the prayer involves a simple "consent" (Pennington, 1999), recognizing that God is active and moving within the inner world, even when we might not "feel" his presence or "get anything" out of the experience. Rather, by consistently turning back to the prayer word, practitioners are cultivating a deeper ability to trust in God, letting go of their own efforts to control what happens next. Over time, this practice may transfer to daily living, with Christians finding that they can apply this gentle, trusting attitude to other areas of life.

The Main Tenets of Centering Prayer

From our perspective, there are a few key, often overlapping ingredients of centering prayer that deserve further attention:

1. Centering prayer is about trusting in God's active, loving presence, beyond words; therefore, the prayer word is simply used as a way to surrender to God, acknowledging that we are letting go of our own efforts. That is, the prayer word is not magical. It does not form a mantra, as in other types of meditation. It is a symbol of our willingness to consent to God in the present moment, focusing exclusively on him in the here and now.
2. Centering prayer is a wordless form of prayer, sitting in silence with God; as a result, we are developing the ability to spend time with God in solitude, letting go of the tendency to use words, thoughts, images, and emotions to guide our relationship with him in these unfolding moments.

3. Centering prayer is about finding rest in God, as Gregory the Great noted; because of this, we are slowing down, allowing the inner world to run its natural course because we are giving over control to God. In finding our rest in God, we are surrendering to God's care for us. We are certain that God loves us, despite an uncertain future.
4. Centering prayer is about reaching out to God in love, rather than knowledge, consistent with *The Cloud of Unknowing*; thus, there will be moments of boredom, doubt, hurt, and so on, given that we are letting go of our own efforts to dictate the pace and timing of God's movements.
5. Centering prayer is about letting go of our own efforts to "reach God," relying instead on God's mercy and grace.
6. Centering prayer is about staying rooted in the present moment, where God is ministering to us, often beyond our conscious awareness.

With the above ingredients in mind, we would like to explore some of the components of this practice in more detail, applying them to your struggle with uncertainty, worry, doubt, and anxiety.

CENTERING PRAYER AND THE FALSE SELF

For Keating (1997), human beings construct a false sense of self throughout the lifespan. Beginning in the first year of life, human beings begin to develop a sense of self that is reliant upon the need for safety, self-worth, and a sense of control and power (Keating, 1997). These three ubiquitous needs, to be sure, can get in the way of living a radical life, rooted in a firm trust in Jesus' active, loving presence.

To begin, all human beings require comfort, security, connection, and safety, with caregivers hopefully responding to these needs in the first few years of life in order to lay a firm psychological foundation. Yet, when these needs are chronically unmet, children go on to be preoccupied with safety, security, and connection, likely because these innate needs were unmet at such an early age. Therefore, in adulthood, some may find that they are constantly searching for someone to offer them the safety they longed for as children.

Children who have not received their due care often have issues with trust. That is, the world is not safe, given that the people that are *supposed* to care for them often do not; therefore, they must rely on themselves to obtain safety. As adults, these children try to attain safety through certainty—having good jobs, living out their dreams, or complying with society's demands to live the American dream. When putting their trust in these earthly treasures, "where moths and vermin destroy, and where thieves break in and steal" (Matthew 6:19), people try harder and harder to find security in a certain future; yet, these are futile attempts at security.

In addition to safety, children crave positive attention, striving to be affirmed and valued during the early years. Eventually, when their needs are responded to, healthy self-esteem develops, resulting in a stable sense of self throughout the lifespan. Recall the words spoken at Jesus' baptism (Matthew 3:17): "This is my Son, whom I love; with him I am well pleased." We all need this loving, blessed attention from our parents, just like Jesus received. Yet, some children are verbally, physically, or sexually abused, resulting in a struggle to see that they were created in God's image with infinite worth. When this happens, life can be filled with disappointment, leading to self-doubt and shame. Over time, adults can end up struggling in work life and intimate relationships, confused about their place in the world.

As the third component of the false self, human beings commonly strive for control, as well as a sense of power within their immediate environment. From the early years of life to our last days, we attempt to maintain at least some control over our personal world. Unfortunately, when human beings do not have a sense of mastery over their surroundings, we may either give up or "double down" in our efforts to secure and maintain control, despite the consequences. In adulthood, this struggle might manifest as intimidation and domination in relationships, or withdrawing from relationships altogether, fearing powerlessness around those we love.

Keating's (1997) three ingredients—security, self-esteem, and power—can definitely get in the way of our relationship with God as well. Based on the notion that the God of the Bible is all-knowing, all-loving, and all-powerful, unilaterally pursuing safety, self-value, and control can lead to disappointment, resentment, and regret. In other words, repeated attempts to attain security, establish a positive sense of self, and have mastery over the internal and external world outside of God ultimately end in failure. As a result, centering prayer can help you to relinquish your grip on these three components of the "false self," allowing you to yield to God's active, loving presence. By letting go and trusting in God's providence, we believe you are preparing yourself to find your identity in him. This newfound reality is in contrast to holding onto your proverbial armor ever so tightly, fearful that reaching out to God will expose you to hurt, disappointment, and danger.

Applying these three ingredients to uncertainty, worry, and anxiety, you might be preoccupied with emotional safety in your life, to the point that following Jesus' plan is perceived as too risky, scary, or unpredictable. Or, you might constantly strive to attain reassurance from others, struggling to trust that loved ones really see your value and intrinsic worth. Relatedly, you might even struggle to trust that God loves you—how could he send his Son to die on a cross for *your* sins, you might ask? Finally, you may constantly strive to control, through sheer power or coercive efforts, most facets of your life because you doubt that you will be able to surrender to God's will from moment to moment.

In the space below, see if you can identify some of your thoughts, feelings, and behaviors surrounding Keating's (1997) "false self," paying particular attention to how these three areas are related to your struggle with uncertainty, worry, and anxiety. Then, following this step, try to journal about what your life would be like (in both your human relationships and your relationship with God) if you were able to simply let go of your "false self," choosing to find your identity in God (rather than unilaterally pursuing safety, self-esteem, and control).

- Safety, comfort, and security:

  _____

  _____

  _____

  _____

  _____

- Self-esteem, value, and worth:

  _____

  _____

  _____

- Power, control, certainty, and predictability:

What would your identity be like if God were the source of your security? If you trusted that God truly cared for you? That God was keeping you safe? That God was comforting you in difficult circumstances?

What would it be like if God said to you, "You are my beloved, I am well pleased with you"?

What would your identity be like if you trusted that God knows what you need, and that he is providentially caring for you? Recall Matthew 6:31–32: "So do not worry, saying, 'What shall we eat?' or 'What shall we drink?' or 'What shall we wear?' For the pagans run after all these things, and your heavenly Father knows that you need them."

What would life be like if you were to hand God your "false self," letting go of your unilateral efforts to attain security, self-worth, and control? What would your human relationships look like? How about your relationship with God? What would you be doing differently, in terms of behaviors, life goals, and so on?

CENTERING PRAYER AND SILENCE

In your busy life, you may find that you have a difficult time sitting in silence for long periods of time. In contemporary society, there is an infinite number of distractions that can pull us away from spending time with God in solitude and silence. Ironically, many people appear busy with emails, texts, and using the Internet, but they are in fact distracting themselves—they are preoccupied (Nouwen, 1981). This preoccupation can deter us from deeper relationships with our sense of self, others, and God. Yet, from our perspective, centering prayer is important for both psychological and spiritual development because it involves stillness and silence, cultivated each day of practice.

Instead of spending one more hour surfing the Internet or binge watching a television show, slowing down enough to recognize that God is moving in the silence is an extremely salient endeavor. As you hit the "brake pedal" of life, you may find that silence is akin to ointment for your anxiety. Rather than using compulsive activity, rumination, worry, and other fast-paced strategies to avoid the pain of life, sitting still (in silence) can help you to fellowship with God on a deeper level.

Although your worrying thoughts and seeds of doubt might continue to manifest, sitting in silence with God (beyond thoughts, feelings, and sensations) can help you to yield to his providence over and over again. By repeatedly letting go, in silence, we believe that you can move in the direction of relinquishing the catastrophic predictions that you "know" will come true. Instead, spending time with Jesus in silence is reminiscent of sitting on the porch with a loved one, gently rocking your chair as you watch the sun set and recognizing that there is no need to say or do anything in the moment.

CENTERING PRAYER AND REST

Relatedly, we believe that centering prayer is about finding rest, slowing down enough to rest in Jesus' arms as you gently return to your prayer word over and over again. Along the way, you may recognize that *your* battle (which is often fought in isolation) with your inner world is actually more exhausting than the thoughts, feelings, and sensations that will not go away. That is, your exhaustion may result from your unilateral efforts to attain security, self-esteem, and control over your own thoughts. To yield to God's sovereign, loving care means that there is nothing you need to do in this very moment, other than utilize your prayer word as a way to say "I surrender, Lord," from moment to moment and from breath to breath.

Because God is all-knowing, all-loving, and all-powerful, there is nowhere else you need to be and nothing else you need to do. What is more, there is nothing you need to do with your inner world, other than simply notice that your worrying, uncertain mind is "at it again." Each time you notice your mind has wandered, you are saying to Jesus, "I give my inner world to you. Do with it what you wish. I trust you." Quietly reciting your prayer word, you are letting go of your own need to solve your problems. You are basking in Jesus' loving embrace from moment to moment. Over time, we believe this act of letting go, gently returning to your prayer word when you have wandered away, can provide you with vital rest.

Again, we suggest that many of your efforts to attain certainty—through worry and "approach" or "avoidance" strategies—are what lead to exhaustion and fatigue. As a result, to fall into God's arms means you are no longer using your own strength, power, or control to generate an outcome that is divorced from him. Rather, God's power can manifest as you acknowledge your weakness, receiving his loving grace in the process (2 Corinthians 12:9).

CENTERING PRAYER, SURRENDER, AND *KENOSIS*

In our view, centering prayer is ideal for your struggle with uncertainty and worry based on the notion that formal practice can help you to cultivate an attitude of self-emptying, consistent with Paul's discussion in his letter to the Philippians (2:5-11):

> In your relationships with one another, have the same mindset as Christ Jesus: Who, being in very nature God, did not consider equality with God something to be used to his own advantage; rather, he *made himself nothing* [italics added] by taking the very nature of a servant, being made in human likeness. And being found in appearance as a man, he humbled himself by becoming obedient to death—even death on a cross! Therefore God exalted him to the highest place and gave him the name that is above every name, that at the name of Jesus every knee should bow, in heaven and on earth and under the earth, and every tongue acknowledge that Jesus Christ is Lord, to the glory of God the Father.

In this passage, the Greek word *kenosis* is used to capture Jesus' self-emptying. However, this self-emptying is not really acknowledging the "true" state of affairs—the idea of *self*, in and of itself, is a fallacy. Rather, the self is emptied in order to be filled for God's purposes.

From our perspective, self-emptying involves humbly letting go of our own efforts to attain certainty, divorced from God's sovereignty. During formal practice, centering prayer can help you to shed your false sense of self, pivoting towards a silent, still state. Within this time, centering prayer can allow you to let God define who you are, given that God is active, present, and moving behind the scenes. In fact, he is even comforting you in the process.

Writing about Jesus' example of self-emptying love while he walked along the paths of life in the first century, Bourgeault (2004) offered the following:

> And he left us a method for practicing this path ourselves, the method he himself modeled to perfection in the garden of Gethsemane. When surrounded by fear, contradiction, betrayal; when the "fight or flight" alarm bells are going off in your head and everything inside you wants to brace and defend itself, the infallible way to extricate yourself and reclaim your home in that sheltering kingdom is simply to

freely release whatever you are holding onto—including, if it comes to this, life itself. The method of full, voluntary self-donation reconnects you instantly to the wellspring; in fact, it is the wellspring. The most daring gamble of Jesus' trajectory of pure love may just be to show us that self-emptying is not the means to something else; the act is itself the full expression of its meaning and instantly brings into being "a new creation": the integral wholeness of Love manifested in the particularity of a human heart. (pp. 87-88)

In your own struggles with uncertainty, doubt, worry, and anxiety, Jesus modeled the way, relinquishing the grip he had on his own life in order to surrender to the will of his Father. In the process, he was "exalted" by the Father. During daily centering prayer, our hope is that you are able to continue to turn to God in your time of need, reminiscent of Jesus' famous saying on the Mount of Olives before his crucifixion (Luke 22:42–44):

"Father, if you are willing, take this cup from me; yet not my will, but yours be done." An angel from heaven appeared to him and strengthened him. And being in anguish, he prayed more earnestly, and his sweat was like drops of blood falling to the ground.

In Luke's account, notice Jesus' attitude of surrender to his Father, letting go of his own will in order to make room for God's plan. Although his Father did not "take the cup" from him, Jesus was "strengthened" by angels so that he may faithfully endure.

In picking up this metaphor of a "cup," Henri Nouwen (1996) described the specific processes, or steps, Christ used in surrendering. First, Christ held the cup in his hands. By this, Christ held the cup by examining its contents, aware of what he had to do. Christ knew that the cross and death were before him, inevitable realities of the mission he came to fulfill. He was also aware that death was not the end for him, holding on to a hope that he would glorify God through his resurrection several days later. In other words, Christ's cup (like ours) was full of *both* sorrow *and* joy, mixed together as he surrendered to God's will for his life. Christ was aware of his fate and the eventual betrayal from his disciples, with whom he had just spent several years walking and sharing life. Next, Christ lifted the cup in order to consume its contents as an act of obedience to God. By lifting (and being lifted up) Christ offered *us* the chance to be with one another and with him. In this sense, lifting the cup was a salute, a "cheers," and an acknowledgment that we are precious creations in God's sight—*imago Dei*—even with our inevitable sorrow and joy. Finally, Christ finished drinking the cup—all the way to the bottom so that it was completely empty. Of course, drinking the entire cup seems to fully capture psychological and spiritual health for devoted Christians—yielding to God's perfect and complete plan.

Within your own life, this attitude of *kenotic* surrendering may allow you to let go of your preoccupation with certainty, using worry to generate a predictable, fixed path outside of God's will. Over time, our hope is that you are able to practice surrender, reminiscent of Jesus in Luke's gospel and Paul's reflections in his letter to the Philippians. We believe that this attitude can help you to find peace in the midst of uncertainty and worry, recognizing that God will strengthen you as he walks by your side on the roads of life. In agreement with Bourgeault (2004), self-emptying is not only a means to an end (ameliorating uncertainty, worry, and anxiety), but a way of life, consistent with Jesus' incarnation. It is how we become Christlike.

CENTERING PRAYER AND RECEPTIVITY

In addition to helping you to let go of the false self, cultivate an inner silence, find rest, and develop an attitude of surrender and self-emptying, we argue that centering prayer can allow you to develop and maintain an open, receptive posture towards God. Rather than solely petitioning God to fix or change your current predicament, centering prayer can help you to "transfer the reins" to God by recognizing that you can trust him in the midst of inner and outer trials. By deepening your ability to maintain a receptive, open "stance" towards God, you are moving in the direction of allowing him to exercise his sovereign plan because he is actively providing for you with his providential care.

CENTERING PRAYER AND THE *APOPHATIC* TRADITION

As noted in the introduction to this chapter, centering prayer has roots in *The Cloud of Unknowing*. Specifically, the anonymous author of *The Cloud of Unknowing* advocated for a wordless, imageless form of prayer, placing all inner experiences beneath a "cloud of forgetting" during contemplative practice. As practitioners relinquish their "knowledge" of God, they look up to a "cloud of unknowing," reaching out to God in love, instead of self-derived knowledge. Within the practice, the author advised practitioners to use a single-syllable word to help them symbolically focus on God, especially during instances of distraction (Bangley, 2006).

Although using words and images in your time spent with God—that is, *kataphatic* prayer—is foundational in the Christian life, we believe that *apophatic* prayer can be especially helpful during instances of uncertainty, worry, doubt, and anxiety. Given that worrying is often about attempting to attain certainty through the use of unilateral cognitive efforts, *apophatic* prayer (practiced via centering prayer) can allow you to relinquish self-derived knowledge, which you may use to predict and control the future. Instead, *apophatic* prayer is about reaching out to God in faithful love, rather than employing human knowledge to understand him. In this process, trust is developed in that you are reaching out to a dark cloud, relying on God's love, mercy, and grace in the process.[1]

Interestingly, the "dark cloud" that *The Cloud of Unknowing* author described is often viewed as a symbol of faith (Johnston, 2000). In other words, instead of using human knowledge to understand God, who is *both* knowable through Jesus Christ *and* beyond our human comprehension, we are letting go of our own efforts, reaching out to God in faith in the process. By employing faith, rather than human-derived reason and knowledge, we are cultivating a deeper reliance on God, who is all-knowing, all-loving, and all-powerful. That is, interior silence allows God to reveal himself to us, instead of us making God in *our* image. In your struggles with uncertainty and worry, this may be the antidote you need, based on the notion that your "stuckness" may involve continuing to try to generate a certain future that will never come. Instead, letting go of worry involves reaching out to God as a "dark cloud," employing faith rather than unilateral efforts that can repeatedly fall short.

CENTERING PRAYER AND COMMON DISTRACTING THOUGHTS

In that centering prayer is a wordless form of prayer, it might be helpful to briefly review several of the most common distracting thoughts that may arise during formal practice. Often overlapping with the central themes of uncertainty, worry, doubt, and future catastrophe, there are at least five types of thoughts that can pull you away from your time spent with God (adapted from Pennington, 1980):

- The "common" thought—These "simple" thoughts consist of an array of words that hover within your mind from moment to moment, often without you even noticing or reflecting on them. These thoughts are the "white noise" that is always on in the background, distracting us and pulling us away from our awareness of God's active, loving presence. During moments of uncertainty and worry, these thoughts may manifest as one word or a group of words, experienced as a steady stream and reminiscent of a waterfall or mountain river.

- The "hooking" thought—Thoughts that seem to "catch" us are notoriously distracting, since they (by definition) pull our attention away from God. Over time, you will hopefully get better at simply noticing these thoughts, before returning to your prayer word with gentleness and compassion. In your daily struggle with uncertainty and worry, the "catching" thought will likely manifest as an idea that you "must" pursue in order to achieve certainty and reduce anxiety. With practice, we believe you will get better at being able to just notice this type of thought, without allowing it to bully you into employing "approach" and "avoidance" strategies to attain a certain future that will probably never come.

- The "monitoring" thought—This type of thought is concerned with your performance, regularly checking in to see how well you are achieving your "goals" during centering prayer. Yet, within formal practice, there is no actual goal, other than to simply rest and allow God to work within you. In other words, you are trusting in faith that God is active and present, rather than turning to your own efforts by striving to somehow "fix" or "improve." With anxiety, you may find yourself trying to "get rid" of uncertainty, worry, and doubt, telling yourself from time to time that you need to do something different because centering prayer is "not working." When this happens, we encourage you to just notice these thoughts, before gently returning to your prayer word to surrender to God's will.

- The "great" idea—With this thought, you may convince yourself you have the answer to a nagging question, or believe that you are able to end your worry through stopping the prayer in order to problem solve, trouble shoot, or check into a solution to a dilemma. Yet, these kinds of thoughts always seem to be present, with centering prayer taking a backseat to your "amazing" thought. This type of thought can be especially convincing when you believe that centering prayer is about achieving a certain state or reducing anxiety. When the "bright idea" arises, we want to encourage you to just notice it, before returning to your prayer word.

- The "distressing" thought—This thought will most certainly emerge during formal practice, and may consist of a theme related to uncertainty or a catastrophe in the future. In fact, your mind will be especially convincing, pulling you away from your prayer word in order to get you to focus on the doomsday scenario that is just around the corner. Unfortunately, this is how the mind works when you are hijacked by uncertainty, worry, doubt, and anxiety. Over time, our hope is that you will get to know the "stressful" thought, acknowledging its presence before returning to your prayer word.

When you experience any of the above thoughts, which may overlap with one another, our suggestion is for you to continue to cultivate an attitude of surrender by letting go of your tendency to pursue them or push them away. Over time, we believe you will get better at recognizing that your mind is just generating thoughts, with the ultimate goal being your surrender to God's providential care. Along the way, you are working on trusting him and putting your faith in his infinite wisdom, love, and power.

Benefits of Centering Prayer: A Psychospiritual Viewpoint

We believe there are several psychological and spiritual benefits to centering prayer. Before offering a brief review of our understanding of the benefits, we believe Pennington's (1980) definition of centering prayer is a useful introduction for this conversation:

> This is what we are seeking in centering prayer: to let go of superficial, false, and limiting constructs and be with who we really are and what we really are: creatures, who come forth from God's love, one with the rest of creation, wholly oriented to finding the fullness of life and love in him; and Christians, who have been given the Christ nature, oriented to be, in Christ, with the Spirit, a complete "yes" to the Father. (p. 123)

What is more, in *Centered Living*, Pennington (1999) highlighted several possible benefits to centering prayer, adapted and expanded upon below:

- Cultivating a deeper relationship with God, who is active and present from moment to moment. Although God has always been present, centering prayer can help practitioners to recognize that he is present, trusting in him and deepening a firm trust in his love. Even in painful moments, God is present as he strengthens our ability to endure. Over time, we can deepen our ability to lean on God's infinite wisdom, love, and power, especially when we are uncertain, worried, and anxious.
- In this burgeoning relationship with God, we are able to recognize that God's infinite love extends to every aspect of our life. To experience God's love from moment to moment means we are able to get through the most ambiguous situations, knowing that God's arms are extended and stretched wide open as he waits patiently for our return (reminiscent of the lost son in Luke 15). In fact, God actively pursues us, consistent with the story of the lost sheep and lost coin that are also in Luke's gospel account.
- Centering prayer can help with tension, given that the act of letting go can help you to find peace in every situation and recognize that God's providential care is permeating each moment. Over time, the practice can help you to cultivate an open, receptive posture. You are regularly inviting God into every second, trusting in his loving, wise, and powerful qualities and attributes.

Beyond Pennington's review, we believe that centering prayer is a good fit for addressing your uncertainty, worry, doubt, and anxiety. If we return to our formal definition of Christian worry, noted below, we see that centering prayer seems to address each component:

> The unsuccessful human attempt, through cognitive efforts, to obtain certainty about an ambiguous future because of the struggle to believe in, trust, and surrender to the perfect care of an infinitely wise, loving, and powerful God.

During formal practice, centering prayer can help you to let go of your own cognitive efforts, given that the practice is *apophatic* by design. In other words, centering prayer is specifically beyond cognition—emphasizing that God is beyond words. Centering prayer is about our experiences, not thoughts. What is more, centering prayer is about surrendering to God, consenting to God's will; therefore, you are letting go of your own efforts to attain certainty. Finally, centering prayer is about trust and faith, allowing God to do the work behind the scenes. Therefore, over time, our hope is that you will deepen your ability to recognize God's attributes, which extend to all of creation. To be sure, God is infinitely wise, loving, and powerful. He is even in control of your inner world. Thus, you can "transfer the reins" to him, relieving yourself of the task of generating certainty on your own. By doing this, you may find an added sense of peace, reminiscent of letting go of the "tug-of-war" rope as you recognize that you do not need to win the battle.

EXERCISE: WHAT ARE YOUR OWN EXPECTATIONS ABOUT CENTERING PRAYER?

Before transitioning to the instructions for centering prayer and the actual daily exercise, see if you can journal for a few minutes about your expectations. Based on the above review, what are you hoping to gain with the daily practice? How can centering prayer help you in your own struggles with uncertainty, worry, doubt, and anxiety? How, if at all, can a more intimate relationship with God help you in your daily struggles? How might the formal practice help you in your daily life, beyond the 20 minutes of practice per day?

___

Instructions for Centering Prayer

As revealed in Keating's (2006) instructions, centering prayer consists of the following four steps:

1. Choose a sacred word as the symbol of your intention to consent to God's presence and action within.

2. Sitting comfortably and with eyes closed, settle briefly and silently introduce the sacred word as the symbol of your consent to God's presence and action within.

3. When engaged with your thoughts, return ever-so-gently to the sacred word.

4. At the end of the prayer period, remain in silence with eyes closed for a couple of minutes. (p. 2)

Exercise: 20-Minute Centering Prayer Meditation

Below is a transcript for the 20-minute exercise (adapted from Keating, 2006), which can also be listened to via the audio file that is available (Track 4 at https://www.routledge.com/Contemplative-Prayer-for-Christians-with-Chronic-Worry-An-Eight-Week-Program/Knabb-Frederick/p/book/9781138690943 under the eResource tab). It is worth mentioning that we have selected the prayer word, "surrender," given that we believe it captures the central aim of contemplative practice within this eight-week program.

- Get into a comfortable position, closing your eyes and sitting up straight in a supportive chair. Gently rest your feet on the floor, and allow your palms to face outward and upward. Rest your hands on your knees or the arms of the chair as your symbolic willingness to let go.
- When you are ready, begin to recite the prayer word, "surrender." Try not to say it too fast or too slow. Instead, just allow the word to repeat itself, serving as your symbolic willingness to yield to God's sovereignty over your inner world. Trusting in him, simply let the word float in your mind, capturing your trust and faith in his infinite love. Just say the word over and over again—"surrender."

- At a certain point, you will recognize that your mind has wandered to another thought, possibly reflective of your uncertainty and worry. When this happens, just notice that your mind has shifted, refocusing on the prayer word. Rather than judging yourself for this pivot away from the prayer word, try to offer yourself loving compassion, non-judgmentally returning to the word. Recognize that God's arms are outstretched, waiting for your return.
- Again and again, just repeat the word, "surrender," acknowledging when your mind has shifted. Continue to sink deeper and deeper into your willingness to surrender to God, letting go of your own efforts to attain certainty and control. As you let go of control, try to just rest in God's arms, recognizing that he is infinitely wise, loving, and powerful. Over and over again, relinquish your own control, letting "surrender" float within your mind. As you say the word, "surrender," you are deepening your ability to trust in his providential care, which extends to all of creation. Because God is active and present, there is nothing you need to do on your part, except symbolically gaze upon him with your prayer word, "surrender."
- As the practice comes to a close, try to just rest in silence for a few moments, before going about your day. If possible, see if you can extend this practice to the rest of your day, yielding to God from moment to moment and trusting in his providential care.

Exercise: Recording Your Daily Efforts for Centering Prayer

In the space that follows, see if you can briefly document your daily experience of centering prayer (beyond what you have documented in the space above).

Day of the Week	Length of Time Practiced (Minutes)	Experience of Uncertainty, Doubt, Worry, and Anxiety Before and After the Practice	Experience of God's Active, Loving Presence Before and After the Practice	Inner Barriers to Centering Prayer (Thoughts, Feelings, and Sensations)	Outer Barriers to Centering Prayer (Distractions in the Environment)
Monday					
Tuesday					
Wednesday					
Thursday					
Friday					
Saturday					
Sunday					

EXERCISE: JOURNALING ABOUT YOUR EXPERIENCE OF CENTERING PRAYER

In the space below, try to journal about your experience of centering prayer on a daily basis (beyond what you have documented in the space above). You may wish to explore your relationship with God, as well as your inner experience of uncertainty, doubt, worry, and anxiety before and after the practice.

Monday

Tuesday

Wednesday

Thursday

Friday

Saturday

Sunday

EXERCISE: HOMEWORK FOR THE WEEK

1. Practice the above 20-minute centering prayer exercise at least once per day for the entire week. Document these experiences in the space provided above.
2. Journal for at least 10 minutes per day about the centering prayer exercise (in the space provided above), focusing on what the experience was like and any potential barriers (e.g., thoughts, feelings, sensations).

RESTING IN GOD'S PRESENCE: REFLECTIONS FROM ERIN, RYAN, AND LISA

In the fifth week of the program, Erin found that she was increasingly able to let go of her own efforts to attain certainty. Through sitting with God in silence, gently repeating "surrender," she found that she was able to find peace in God's presence. She was also able to trust that he was there in the midst of her pain. Instead of clinging to a false self, organized around her unilateral attempts to achieve safety and comfort, Erin was able to reach for God over and over again by putting her faith in his power and love.

With Ryan, the fifth week consisted of deepening his ability to yield to God's infinite wisdom, "surrendering" to God's providential care. Although he still experienced thoughts of doubt and uncertainty, he found that centering prayer helped him to recognize when these thoughts distracted him from God's active, loving presence. Ryan was especially drawn to the quiet, looking forward to formal practice, given that he did not have to "do" anything. Rather, he was able to rest, trusting that God would provide.

In Lisa's experience, God was moving and active in the fifth week of the program. Instead of using "approach" strategies to generate a sense of certainty and predictability, she noticed that she was able to "let go," trusting that God would illuminate her paths. In spite of the fact that she continued to struggle with uncertainty, worry, and anxiety, she found that *kenotic* self-emptying really helped her in these moments, pivoting her towards putting her faith in God's love. Relinquishing her own efforts to secure a certain future, she looked forward to the moments in her day that involved resting in God's arms.

CONCLUSION

Building on prior weeks, the fifth week consisted of continuing to cultivate a deeper sense of trust in God, shedding your own efforts to pursue control. Instead, our hope is that you were able to find some peace in spending time with God, beyond words. Pivoting from the pursuit of knowledge to a loving, experiential way of knowing, we believe that centering prayer can allow you to develop a firm trust in God's active, loving presence from moment to moment. In the next chapter, you will continue to practice centering prayer, focusing on the contemplative attitudes that are developed in this wordless, silent time spent with God.

NOTE

1 See Johnston (2000) for a detailed review of the central themes of *The Cloud of Unknowing*, including those presented in this paragraph.

REFERENCES

Bangley, B. (2006). *The Cloud of Unknowing: Contemporary English Edition*. Brewster, MA: Praclete Press.
Bourgeault, C. (2004). *Centering Prayer and Inner Awakening*. New York: Cowley Publications.
Johnston, W. (2000). *The Mysticism of the Cloud of Unknowing*. New York: Fordham University Press.
Keating, T. (1997). *Invitation to Love: The Way of Christian Contemplation*. New York: The Continuum Publishing Company.
Keating, T. (2006). *The Method of Centering Prayer: The Prayer of Consent*. Butler, NJ: Contemplative Outreach, Ltd.
Nouwen, H. (1981). *Making All Things New: An Invitation to the Spiritual Life*. San Francisco, CA: HarperSanFrancisco.
Nouwen, H. (1996). *Can You Drink the Cup?* Notre Dame, IN: Ave Maria Press, Inc.
Pennington, B. (1980). *Centering Prayer: Renewing an Ancient Christian Prayer Form*. New York: Doubleday.
Pennington, B. (1999). *Centered Living: The Way of Centering Prayer*. Liguori, MO: Liguori Publications.
Pennington, B., & Keating, T. (2007). *Finding Grace at the Center: The Beginnings of Centering Prayer*. Woodstock, VT: Skylight Paths Publishing.

Week 6

A CONTINUATION OF CENTERING PRAYER

Introduction

This week, you will continue with your practice of centering prayer, given that we believe the practice can help you surrender to God's providence during instances of uncertainty, worry, doubt, and anxiety. When you are preoccupied with future catastrophe, you might find that you are especially paralyzed, struggling to live the life you want. Therefore, we suggest that formal practice—20 minutes at a time, at least once per day—can be helpful in translating the benefits to daily life. In the process, you will be developing several "contemplative attitudes" (Frenette, 2012), or, as the Apostle Paul talked about it, the mindset of Christ (Philippians 2:5).

Building on (and overlapping with) the last chapter, you will learn about some of the more popular "contemplative attitudes" (Frenette, 2012) that are cultivated in centering prayer, including the ability to be open and to live a simple life because of your awareness of God's active, loving presence. In addition, deepening your ability to approach life with a gentle receptivity is especially important, finding rest in God and simply "being" within each moment. It is the ability to be open to God, moment by moment, which allows us to surrender to God's presence—the Christian antidote to worry and uncertainty.

These attitudes (adapted from Frenette, 2012; Chryssavgis, 2008) are relevant in your daily struggle with uncertainty, worry, and anxiety, based on the notion that centering prayer can help you to change the way you relate to the inner world by inviting God into the process. Instead of trying to somehow control your thoughts and feelings, centering prayer can allow you to "detach" from your preoccupation with these inner events, pivoting to God as you reach out to him for comfort, security, and safety. As Foster (2011) reminds us, the idea is not to empty the mind of meaningless attachments; instead, we desire to be filled with the mind of Christ. Although your future will never be fully knowable, partnering with God can help you to trust in his wisdom, goodness, and power, shedding the distractions that pull you away from his presence.

In fact, one of the most powerful components of contemplative practice in general, and centering prayer in particular, is the ability to develop a "spirit of poverty," "freedom," and "detachment" (Burton-Christie, 1993; Chryssavgis, 2008), consistent with Jesus' teaching on worry (Matthew 6:25–34). Because God's providence is guiding his creation, Christians can let go of their preoccupation with tomorrow, relinquishing the grip they have on unilateral attempts to attain certainty. In other words, our preoccupation with our own wants and needs is ultimately a distraction from God. As Nouwen (1981) reminds us, we are "filled but unfulfilled" (p. 8).

We try to attain certainty by filling our schedules with extraneous activities. By trusting in God's providential care, though, we no longer need to focus on attaining certainty for ourselves—we trust in God's care for us.

Among the early desert Christians, a foundational goal was freedom from a variety of distractions that got in the way of yielding to God (Burton-Christie, 1993). Certainly, the early Christians who transitioned to desert life to be with God experienced a wide variety of inner and outer events that pulled their attention away from God as their source of life. Yet, over time, they were able to cultivate a deeper trust in him, purposely letting go of all of the barriers—possessions, thoughts, feelings, memories, distractions, and so on—to a deeper union with God.

Because of the importance of this "spirit of poverty," we will be reviewing the many ways in which centering prayer can help you to surrender to God's loving presence from moment to moment, culminating with the ability to more closely resemble Jesus in his willingness to yield to his Father's will (captured in the gospels). As Jesus revealed, the most important part of life is to drink the cup that God offers (Luke 22:42), moving towards aligning our will with his unique plan for our life.

Centering Prayer and Consenting to God

As noted in the directions for centering prayer, the short word ("surrender," for example, is the word used in this eight-week program) serves as a symbol of our willingness to "consent" (Frenette, 2012). But what, exactly, are we "consenting" to? In essence, the word captures our willingness to allow God to work within our innermost being, letting him do what he wants to do with our thoughts and feelings. In this process, we defer to God's direction in bringing up experiences—those we may delight in as well as those that may be uncomfortable. We trust that God, as the Good Physician, is with us in the experience—leading, guiding, and healing. In this process, of course, there is an assumption that God is *already* moving, rather than disengaged, aloof, and passively watching from some distant heaven.

It is important to remember that consent, or surrender, is not a passive process by any means. Surrender is an active one, given that we are making the choice to let go. In fact, centering prayer allows us to be attentively engaged with the subtle, nuanced activity of God's spirit in our lives, including our inner experiences. Further, the prayer word symbolically represents our conscious decision to be with God (not fight against God) in the process. Our consent is created by having "an attitude of waiting upon the Lord with loving attentiveness" (Keating, 2014, p. 43). In our inner stillness, we learn to patiently wait for God to show up, even when we might not "feel" him. It is in waiting that we learn to collaborate with God by consenting to his direction and his leading, trusting in him in the process.

Just as we might take for granted that our heart is beating, acknowledging that God is already present and ministering to our unconscious can feel quite foreign and be outside of our spiritual awareness. Yet, as St. Augustine powerfully declared, "God is closer to us than we are to ourselves." As we repeatedly "consent" to his active presence, trusting that he is with us and meeting our needs from moment to moment within our inner world, we are slowly learning to relinquish our own efforts to control and predict the future.

Stated differently, as we "let go" of our own control efforts, unilaterally striving to manage our thoughts and feelings, we are learning to simply observe—to acknowledge our experiences and put our faith in God's presence to orchestrate and guide our inner being. This practice, when cultivated through centering prayer, can help us to develop an inner peace, even in the midst of the storms of life.

Remember that this type of prayer invites us to recognize God as the active agent in this process (Foster, 2011). We utilize our imagination in observing all of our experiences, not simply trying to avoid certain experiences and attain other ones. Therefore, when you are feeling especially anxious, worrying to generate certainty, centering prayer can allow you to simply "consent." You are acknowledging that God is sovereign over your inner world and that there is nothing else you need to do in this moment.

CENTERING PRAYER AND OPENNESS

Beyond "consenting" to God's active, loving presence, centering prayer can help you to develop an open inner posture towards God (Frenette, 2012). By "openness," we mean that you are transitioning from being guarded, closed off, and protected to being willing to receive and truly see God's active presence in both the world and within the depths of your being. To relate this topic to the physical world, holding your hands tightly shut signifies control, with humans constantly striving to maintain some sort of autonomy and power over our immediate environment. Still, when we are able to open our hands, with our palms facing the sky, we are preparing ourselves to receive God's mercy and grace. These gifts from God have already been fully, completely offered by Jesus on the cross: "It is finished" (John 19:30).

Both psychologically and spiritually, this receptive posture can help you to more fully trust in God because you are placing your faith in his hands. Openness, therefore, is a disposition for seeing God's hand in all of life's events, even within your thoughts and feelings. Recall the garden of Gethsemane scene in Matthew 26. Matthew 26:39 states: "Going a little farther, he fell with his face to the ground and prayed, 'My Father, if it is possible, may this cup be taken from me. Yet not as I will, but as you will.'" The image reflected here is one of openness. Jesus did not wish to go to the cross; however, he trusted in God's providential will. Jesus was perfectly aware of his experience—*not wanting* the experience. In fact, Matthew recorded Jesus praying for deliverance from this reality several times. Still, Jesus was open to the will of God—not *my* will, but "as *you* will" (italics added). Because he is sovereign, maintaining an open stance towards God involves acknowledging what is already a reality—because God is infinitely wise, good, and powerful, he orchestrates *all* of life.

To stand back and allow God to work—welcoming in his loving presence—is especially salient for your daily struggle with uncertainty and worry, based on the notion that your unilateral control strategies have likely failed to produce lasting results. Although you have probably tried on your own to solve your own anticipated future catastrophes, God is patiently waiting for you to fall into his loving arms. To fall, though, requires an openness to the reality that his arms are already there. By consenting to God via your prayer word, you are learning to remain receptive to this reality.

CENTERING PRAYER AND THE SIMPLE LIFE

In addition to the ability to consent to God in an open fashion, centering prayer is about slowing down to embrace the simple aspects of your faith (Frenette, 2012). As you carve out daily time to sit with God in silence, you are learning to find rest in him in one of the most simplistic ways possible. Rather than getting swept away by the busyness of a complex, complicated world, you are stating to God, "This time with you in silence is enough for me." For James Finley (2004), a popular contemplative writer and clinical psychologist, Jesus' ability to surrender to God's will is especially reflective of the simple life, recognizing that God is active and present within even the most basic, stripped-down experiences of daily living:

The Gospels tell us of how Jesus abandoned himself to the Father's will in the big picture of his own unfolding life. But Jesus gave witness to a more finely tuned awareness of God's providential presence revealed to us in the way Jesus saw the flowers of the field or the birds of the air or a small child climbing up into his lap. In meditation we imitate Christ by abandoning ourselves to the providential flow of such *simple* [italics added] and concrete things as the sound of children who happen to be playing outside the window. Sitting still and straight, we remain present, open, and awake to the providential flow of the sound of the clock chiming, just now, on the mantel. We abandon ourselves to the utterly trustworthy providential flow of the room in which we sit as it darkens at sunset. We sit abandoned to the providential flow of our own breathing, to the thought passing, just now, through our mind. We sit surrendered to the divinity flowing through the never-quite-this-way-before, never-quite-this-way-again immediacy of the moment just as it is. (p. 29)

Notice, here, that we are able to slow down to experience the simple, life-giving moments along our journey when we are aware of God's providential hand, which guides even the most miniscule details of daily life. Instead of being swept away by thoughts of uncertainty and feelings of fear and anxiety, we are able to lean down and experience a sense of awe in watching ants scurry about on an anthill or look up to the sky to watch a flock of birds fly by in a particular pattern. In your own life, try to think about what your world might be like if you were able to passionately connect to each moment, aware that God is pushing things along and attending to the details of the planet that he created when he spoke those famous words in the first chapter of Genesis: "Let there be . . ."

Certainly, simplicity seems to be an especially fitting antidote for uncertainty and worry, given that we are not consumed by the "What if . . . ?" game. Instead, we are allowing God to provide, trusting that his providential care effortlessly flows from his hand. As this happens, we are able to experience the world with a sense of mystery and awe, praising God for giving us the opportunity to interact with his well-designed creation. To simplify life, therefore, involves allowing worrying thoughts and anxious feelings to run their natural course, acknowledging that God holds each passing moment in the palm of his hand.

By repeatedly consenting to God, trusting that he is active and present as we repeat our prayer word, we are learning to lean on him in a simple manner. We are divorced from our convoluted attempts to predict the future and attain a certain outcome for an event that might not even happen. Instead of being lost in our head, playing the "What if . . . ?" game, we are able to hit the brake pedal of life to notice the scenery, recognizing that speeding through life, solely trying to avoid dangerous towns and treacherous landscapes, is by no means truly living.

CENTERING PRAYER AND A GENTLER APPROACH TO LIFE

Along the roads of life, centering prayer can help us be a bit gentler in the way we respond to the thoughts and feelings that pass through our inner world and our fellow human beings, displaying less effort as we connect to God's mercy and grace from moment to moment (Frenette, 2012). In other words, as we transfer formal practice to daily life, we utilize a lighter touch when interacting with the world, recognizing that God is ultimately in control. As a result, we are less inclined to exert all of our *own* effort and strength to get through the day.

There are so many images of Jesus interacting with others in a gentle fashion. Perhaps one of the most famous is Jesus' interaction with the woman committing adultery. In John 8:3–5, we read:

The teachers of the law and the Pharisees brought in a woman caught in adultery. They made her stand before the group and said to Jesus, "Teacher, this woman was caught in the act of adultery. In the Law Moses commanded us to stone such women. Now what do you say?"

Jesus understood that the teachers and Pharisees were not interested in punishing this woman, but wanted to set a trap for Jesus. Next, Jesus began writing something in the dirt. He eventually said (John 8:7), "Let any one of you who is without sin be the first to throw a stone at her." Those in attendance eventually left, choosing not to stone her for her acts because of their own imperfect histories, with only Jesus and the woman remaining behind. Jesus then told the woman that he did not condemn her. Talk about a merciful response on Jesus' part. Jesus' gentleness was intimately connected with his insight into the experiences of others.

When daily practice turns into weekly and monthly practice, we are learning to be gentle because God is ministering to our needs. As Keating (2014) revealed, the more time spent in centering prayer, the more negative experiences will usually surface. This is because centering prayer opens up space for God to gently heal these difficult inner events. Because of this, we are more likely to allow God to lead the way, recognizing that all of the unilateral striving is in vain. To relate this gentle, effortless approach to uncertainty and worry, we believe that so much of the struggle with anxiety is about the human attempt to generate a predictable, knowable, and controllable future. Of course, given that life is chaotic, this day will never arrive. Therefore, the sooner we are able to fall into God's arms, trusting that he is leading the way, the more quickly we will shed our autonomous pseudo-strength.

Centering Prayer and Relinquishing Your Grip

In our efforts to gently interact with God's creation by giving up our own willpower to make it on our own, we may find that we can let go of the tight grip we have on an ambiguous, uncertain future. In other words, as you learn to sit with God in silence, trusting that he is ministering to you beyond words, thoughts, images, and feelings, you may begin to notice how tired your hands are because of all of the clutching, grasping, and tightening you have been engaged in. To let go (Frenette, 2012) thus means that you are no longer preoccupied with holding on to the thing you never truly possessed—an omniscient, omnipotent mastery over the future. For the purposes of struggling with uncertainty, our ability to attain any meaningful certainty outside of our relationship with God will ultimately fall short.

In your daily practice, you may find that letting go offers you added peace and comfort, knowing that God is orchestrating the world in which you interact and live. Rather than trying to be all-knowing and all-powerful, you might be especially drawn to the notion that your perceived grip no longer serves its purpose. You have a guide who is one step ahead of you, illuminating the potholes in the road. In your 20-minute daily practice, consenting to God's will by putting your faith in his active presence (even when you do not "feel" him) can help you to begin to rest in *his* sovereign arms.

Centering Prayer and Rest

Reminiscent of standing on your feet for long periods of time followed by the opportunity to sit down and "take a load off," you may find that daily centering prayer can help you to rest in God's presence (Frenette, 2012). Because there is no need for you to "do" anything—after all, you are relying solely on his grace and mercy—a central aim of centering prayer is for you to slow down enough to open yourself to his loving comfort. Again and again, centering prayer is about pausing to open yourself to him, recognizing that there is nothing you can "do." In the process, you are shedding all of your clever tricks, coping skills, defenses, and distractions. Rather, in this very moment, your prayer word symbolizes your surrender. You are "waving the white flag" as you say to God,

"I've tried to control things again. Help me to rely on you, rather than my own efforts. You are sovereign, loving, and wise, which is enough for me."

In Matthew's gospel (11:28–30), Jesus famously stated the following:

> Come to me, all you who are weary and burdened, and I will give you rest. Take my yoke upon you and learn from me, for I am gentle and humble in heart, and you will find rest for your souls. For my yoke is easy and my burden is light.

With centering prayer, you are asking to cast your burdens, aches, and pains onto Jesus, surrendering to his divine providence. As you repeat the word "surrender," you are asking God to work within your innermost being, healing you and comforting you in your time of need.

This form of prayer may even make room for more and more negative experiences to surface. Keating's (2014) term for this component of centering prayer is "unloading" (p. 46), which occurs because difficult thoughts, feelings, and sensations have been opened up as we increasingly learn to rest in God's loving presence. In other words, more interior space is available for distracting thoughts, painful feelings, and traumatic images, experiences that can function as barriers to a deeper, more loving and trusting relationship with God (Keating, 2014). Ultimately, centering prayer can help us come to the realization that: (a) these difficult, often confusing and distracting inner experiences are only a small part of a larger experience (with God located at the center); and (b) God is active throughout these distressing experiences, even when they are chronic and enduring and we may be confused about their meaning in the grand scheme of things (Keating, 2014). In that Jesus is gentle and humble, he *will* respond, offering you much-needed psychological and spiritual rest. Trusting in this reality, in turn, can help you to let go of your unilateral efforts to achieve certainty through chronic worry.

CENTERING PRAYER AND THE ABILITY TO JUST "BE"[1]

By finding rest in God through centering prayer, you may find you are able to simply "be," rather than constantly striving to perform, manage, fix, and so on (Frenette, 2012). Given that these efforts to attain certainty and control have likely fallen short of their goal of the total elimination of ambiguity, you might currently be feeling exhausted. To just "be," therefore, is about handing over control to God, recognizing that your role in your relationship with him is to trust him. Simply put, you are placing your faith in his providential care. Rather than constantly trying to pursue a "fix it on my own" approach to life, centering prayer can help you to move from being the "tour guide" to being the "vacationer."

As you learn to simply "be," you may find that you are able to enjoy life on a deeper level, coming to the realization that you were never truly able to control day-to-day living anyway. In this process, you may end up feeling an added sense of peace, reminiscent of watching nature. For many individuals who enjoy spending time in nature, one of the benefits is that they are able to just watch, without needing to "do" anything. From watching a sunset to observing a squirrel carry an acorn up a tree, the goal is to allow what is in front of you to simply unfold, recognizing that you play no role in "controlling" nature. Stated differently, nature will continue to function, regardless of whether or not you are "intervening" to somehow move it along.

In a similar vein, when walking along the roads of life, God is orchestrating the day-to-day events that you encounter; therefore, centering prayer can help you to relinquish the grip you have on daily living, coming to the realization that it was never your job to control the world in which you live anyway. Rather, because God is infinitely wise, good, and powerful, you can faithfully trust that he has your best intentions in mind. This form of "being," to be sure, can help you in your moments of uncertainty, worry, doubt, and anxiety. Your main job is to acknowledge what has always been true—God is helping you along, and will continue to provide for you, illuminating your paths and intervening in your life because he loves you.

Since God's grace has covered over your past—which is filled with shortcomings, mistakes, and so on—and because God's providential care is guiding your future, you can let go of both ruminations and worries. Slowly, you may come to grips with the notion that your job in the present moment is to look to him. In formal practice, centering prayer can help you to repeatedly let go, focusing on "being" in the moment because God is active, present, and healing your innermost being. Although you might not always "feel" his presence, centering prayer as an *apophatic* form of prayer can help you to let go of your own cognitive, language-based efforts to control and predict the future. As a way to repeatedly turn from self-sufficiency, autonomy, and unilateral attempts to carve out your own path with a sense of predictability and certainty, centering prayer can help you to cultivate an attitude of "being" during key moments of uncertainty and anxiety.

Of course, we are by no means suggesting that simply "being" will work in all situations. After all, life is also about taking action when it is possible and necessary to do so. Yet, when it comes to uncertainty and anxiety, you may find that your "approach" or "avoidance" strategies are derailing your life. In fact, they may be getting in the way of you enjoying what is in front of you, whether you are watching a sunset, spending time with your children or other loved ones, or trying to focus on a hobby or task in order to give your best effort. Above all else, simply "being" when you do not have control is the best option, with formal practice helping you to transfer the benefits of centering prayer to both big and small events. Consistent with watching the snow outside your window, you can just let the world unfold, acknowledging that you have no control over whether or not the clouds, temperature, and other environmental events will be functioning in such a way as to produce the snowflakes that are effortlessly falling to the ground.

Interestingly, the third chapter of Ecclesiastes seems to best capture the importance of turning to God in life, with King Solomon (the possible author) offering a long list of events in life to highlight God's sovereignty:

> There is a time for everything, and a season for every activity under the heavens: a time to be born and a time to die, a time to plant and a time to uproot, a time to kill and a time to heal, a time to tear down and a time to build, a time to weep and a time to laugh, a time to mourn and a time to dance, a time to scatter stones and a time to gather them, a time to embrace and a time to refrain from embracing, a time to search and a time to give up, a time to keep and a time to throw away, a time to tear and a time to mend, a time to be silent and a time to speak, a time to love and a time to hate, a time for war and a time for peace. What do workers gain from their toil? I have seen the burden God has laid on the human race. He has made everything beautiful in its time. He has also set eternity in the human heart; yet no one can fathom what God has done from beginning to end. I know that there is nothing better for people than to be happy and to do good while they live. That each of them may eat and drink, and find satisfaction in all their toil—this is the gift of God. I know that everything God does will endure forever; nothing can be added to it and nothing taken from it. God does it so that people will fear him.

In this passage within the Hebrew Bible, we see that God's actions "endure forever," and that there is no human action that "can be added" or "taken from" God's plan. In our view, in your uncertainty, worry, doubt, and anxiety, there is a time for "being" and a time for "acting." With centering prayer, you are learning that there is a time for "being," recognizing that God's enduring actions are all you need in the present moment.

CENTERING PRAYER AND GOD'S LOVING ARMS

As you move in the direction of "being" in key moments of uncertainty, worry, and anxiety, we believe you will increasingly recognize that God is holding you in his arms; in fact, he has *always* been doing so over the course of your life (Frenette, 2012). In other words, rather than seeing yourself as isolated and on your own, needing to unilaterally come up with solutions to future predicaments, God is sustaining you and providing for you. As a result, you can simply fall into his arms, reminiscent of the lost son being embraced by his father as he headed back home, acknowledging that he could not continue on (Luke 15:11–32).

Similarly, centering prayer is about resting in God's loving arms, acknowledging that *he* is doing the work. Beyond the story of the lost son, centering prayer is consistent with the story of both the lost sheep and the lost coin (Luke 15:1–10), given that you are passively letting God pursue you during formal practice. Because God is active and you are letting go of control, and because God is infinitely wise, good, and powerful, you can put your faith in his ways. To reach out to God—in love rather than knowledge—means that you are trusting that his outstretched arms have been there all along. Your role, in turn, is to simply recognize what has already been there during this form of silent, wordless prayer.

CENTERING PRAYER AND "DETACHMENT"

One of the most important aspects of the spiritual development of early desert Christians was the ability to achieve freedom from both inner distractions and outer events. In particular, desert monks sought freedom from a wide variety of worldly cares (adapted from Burton-Christie, 1993):

- Freedom from worry, anxiety, and a preoccupation with an unknown future.
- Freedom from painful memories and distractions from prior life events.
- Freedom from an unhealthy over-identification with the autonomous self; this self-focused style, to be sure, can get in the way of lasting, deeply fulfilling connections with both God and other humans.
- Freedom from a wide variety of "cares," which monks were able to "cast on the Lord" (Psalm 55:22).

To apply this freedom to your own life, try to reflect on what your life might be like if you were able to let go of your struggle with worrying about the future and ruminating about the past, surrendering your catastrophic predictions and painful memories to God. What is more, how might your life be different if you attained an inner freedom from the grip that your false sense of self has had on you? What if you were able to shift towards loving others in the context of a supportive, faith-based community, "casting your cares on the Lord" in the process?

Through formal centering prayer, we believe you are planting seeds that will sprout during informal daily living. Even in this sowing, remember Jesus' words in Matthew 6:26: "Look at the birds of the air; they do not sow or reap or store away in barns, and yet your heavenly Father feeds them. Are you not much more valuable than they?" We faithfully engage in the practice, trusting that God is in control of *both* the process *and* the outcome. We cannot make the seeds grow. We can only plant them.

In other words, as you consent to God's will in silence and stillness, we are hopeful that you will extend this attitude—saying "yes" to God from moment to moment and "no" to chasing your own certainty, divorced from his plans—to the days, weeks, months, and years that lie ahead. Over time, "detaching" from the cares of the world, reminiscent of Jesus' teaching on worry in Matthew's gospel (6:25–34), can free you up to live the life you have only dreamed of, trusting in God's providential care as you place one foot in front of the other on the paths of life.

CENTERING PRAYER, THE CONTEMPLATIVE ATTITUDES, AND JESUS

In our reading of the gospel accounts of Jesus' life, we argue that Jesus exemplified many of the contemplative attitudes presented in this chapter. In fact, within the gospel of John, Jesus' unique relationship with his Father was especially emphasized (Kostenberger, 2009). As Jesus faced his inevitable execution, he yielded to his Father's will, "drinking the cup" that his Father prepared for him. Along the way, he recognized that his divine purpose on this planet was to consent to God's will, opening up to God's presence within the three decades he walked the earth. In a simple and gentle manner, he followed God's plan for his life, detaching from everything else.

We also point to Paul's emphasis on having a mindset like Christ's (Philippians 2:5–11). The critical component of this mindset is emptying, or *kenosis* in Greek. Philippians 2:6–8 reads:

> [Jesus], being in very nature God, did not consider equality with God something to be used to his own advantage; rather, *he made himself nothing* [*kenosis*; italics added] by taking the very nature of a servant, being made in human likeness. And being found in appearance as a man, he humbled himself by becoming obedient to death—even death on a cross!

As Gorman (2009) emphasized, the idea of giving up, or emptying, does not point to some sort of loss of identity by any means. In other words, with his incarnation, Christ did not somehow lose his position within the Trinity. Instead, he became a servant, obediently fulfilling his final mission after three decades on this planet. In a counterintuitive manner, this passage explicates that God's divine nature is in no way exploitive; instead, Jesus' divine purpose is all about self-emptying and obedience, truly embodied within the atonement, which powerfully reconciles humankind to God (Gorman, 2009). Certainly, the cross reveals both God's "true divinity" and the potential for "true humanity," with this passage equating *kenosis* and obedience with Christ's self-sacrifice (Gorman, 2009).

In centering prayer, we are fostering a sense of increased Christlikeness within the inner world. Recall from previous chapters that this focus is called *theosis*. In line with Gorman (2009), we argue that "*kenosis* is *theosis*" (p. 37). When reading Philippians 2, we see that God's most authentic form is all about self-emptying and obedience. This obedience to the point of death on a cross becomes the truest expression of humanity. "God is not a god of power *and* weakness, but the God of power *in* weakness" (Gorman, 2009, p. 33, italics in original). Christ's obedience and surrender to God's will forms the context of our own Christian spirituality. We become Christlike as we empty ourselves and surrender to God's will. Again, an important practice for this is centering prayer.

Interestingly, Jesus instructed his disciples to also yield to the will of God, teaching them a simple, powerful prayer (Matthew 6:9–13):

> Our Father in heaven, hallowed be your name, your kingdom come, your will be done, on earth as it is in heaven. Give us today our daily bread. And forgive us our debts, as we also have forgiven our debtors. And lead us not into temptation, but deliver us from the evil one.

Within this famous prayer, Jesus advocated for God's will to be done, helping his disciples to simplify matters by asking God for basic necessities, forgiveness, and deliverance. In this concise prayer, Jesus was teaching his followers to trust in God's goodness, mercy, grace, and infinite wisdom, given that God's will is what is best for his creation.

As you reflect on this short prayer, see if you can ponder what your life would be like if you were able to slow down enough to: (a) submit to God's will; (b) trust that his will is best for your life; (c) recognize that God will provide for you; and (d) believe that God has already forgiven you for your mistakes and stumbles, clearing your debt when you have missed the mark and looking out for your future steps in his ability to protect you from harm.

To relate Jesus' prayer to centering prayer, both are focused on consenting to God's will, allowing those who say the words with an authentic fervor to trust in God's plan. Both simplify life by allowing you to trust that God will meet basic needs and offer forgiveness. Reminiscent of both Jesus' prayer and centering prayer, surrendering to God is paramount within the Christian life, especially when considering psychological and spiritual health. By yielding to his infinite wisdom, goodness, and power, you are shifting from autonomy, self-sufficiency, and isolation to a union like no other, captured perfectly via the atonement. As Jesus obediently walked to the cross, his primary aim was to carry out the will of his Father, reconciling humankind to God because it is in God's nature to care for, and respond to, his creation.

INSTRUCTIONS FOR CENTERING PRAYER: A REVIEW

To offer a review of Keating's (2006) instructions, first presented in the last chapter, centering prayer consists of four key steps during formal practice:

1. Choose a sacred word as the symbol of your intention to consent to God's presence and action within.
2. Sitting comfortably and with eyes closed, settle briefly and silently introduce the sacred word as the symbol of your consent to God's presence and action within.
3. When engaged with your thoughts, return ever-so-gently to the sacred word.
4. At the end of the prayer period, remain in silence with eyes closed for a couple of minutes. (p. 2)

EXERCISE: CONTINUING WITH THE 20-MINUTE CENTERING PRAYER MEDITATION

Below is a transcript for the 20-minute exercise (adapted from Keating, 2006), which is the same as in the last chapter and can be listened to via the audio file that is available (Track 4 at https://www.routledge.com/Contemplative-Prayer-for-Christians-with-Chronic-Worry-An-Eight-Week-Program/Knabb-Frederick/p/book/9781138690943 under the eResource tab).

- Get into a comfortable position, closing your eyes and sitting up straight in a supportive chair. Gently rest your feet on the floor. Allow your palms to face outward and upward, resting on your knees or the arms of the chair as your symbolic willingness to let go.
- When you are ready, begin to recite the prayer word, "surrender." Try not to say it too fast or too slow. Instead, just allow the word to repeat itself, serving as your symbolic willingness to yield to God's sovereignty over your inner world. Trusting in him, simply let the word float in your mind, capturing your trust and faith in his infinite love. Just say the word over and over again—"surrender."

A CONTINUATION OF CENTERING PRAYER

- At a certain point, you will recognize that your mind has wandered to another thought. This thought may reflect your uncertainty and worry. When this happens, just notice that your mind has shifted, and then refocus on the prayer word. Rather than judging yourself for this pivot away from the prayer word, try to offer yourself loving compassion, non-judgmentally returning to the word. Recognize that God's arms are outstretched, waiting for your return.

- Again and again, just repeat the word, "surrender," acknowledging when your mind has shifted. Continue to sink deeper and deeper into your willingness to surrender to God, letting go of your own efforts to attain certainty and control. As you let go of control, try to just rest in God's arms, recognizing that he is infinitely wise, loving, and powerful. Over and over again, relinquish your own control, letting "surrender" float within your mind. As you say the word, "surrender," you are deepening your ability to trust in his providential are, which extends to all of creation. Because God is active and present, there is nothing you need to do on your part, except symbolically gaze upon him with your prayer word, "surrender."

- As the practice comes to a close, try to just rest in silence for a few moments, before going about your day. If possible, see if you can extend this practice to the rest of your day, yielding to God from moment to moment and trusting in his providential care.

EXERCISE: CONTINUING TO RECORD YOUR DAILY EFFORTS FOR CENTERING PRAYER

Consistent with the last chapter, in the space that follows, see if you can briefly document your daily experience of centering prayer (beyond what you have documented in the space above).

Day of the Week	Length of Time Practiced (Minutes)	Experience of Uncertainty, Doubt, Worry, and Anxiety Before and After the Practice	Experience of God's Active, Loving Presence Before and After the Practice	Inner Barriers to Centering Prayer (Thoughts, Feelings, and Sensations)	Outer Barriers to Centering Prayer (Distractions in the Environment)
Monday					
Tuesday					
Wednesday					
Thursday					
Friday					
Saturday					
Sunday					

EXERCISE: CONTINUING TO JOURNAL ABOUT YOUR EXPERIENCE OF CENTERING PRAYER

Similar to the last chapter, in the space below, try to journal about your experience of centering prayer on a daily basis (beyond what you have documented in the space above). You may wish to explore your relationship with God, as well as your inner experience of uncertainty, doubt, worry, and anxiety before and after the practice.

Monday

Tuesday

Wednesday

A Continuation of Centering Prayer

Thursday

Friday

Saturday

Sunday

Exercise: Homework for the Week

1. Similar to the last week, practice the above 20-minute centering prayer exercise at least once per day for the entire week. Document your experiences in the space provided above.
2. Consistent with the last week, journal for at least 10 minutes per day about the centering prayer exercise (in the space provided above), focusing on what the experience was like and any potential barriers (e.g., thoughts, feelings, sensations).

CONCLUSION

In this chapter, you were able to continue to practice centering prayer, recognizing that many of the "contemplative attitudes" are about learning to simply "be" with God. In the process, you are letting go of your own tendencies to control, predict, and manage the future. Instead, centering prayer is about "being," shifting from "doing" because God is infinitely wise, loving, and powerful. He is providentially carving out the best possible path for your life. In the next chapter, you will continue to build on your practice of centering prayer with the welcoming prayer, a form of prayer that was developed as a way to extend centering prayer to daily life. You will be inviting God into your pain in the process.

NOTE

1   Interestingly, Segal et al. (2012) have also highlighted the "being" mode, contrasting this attitude towards inner events with the "doing" mode. These two modes will be discussed further in the next chapter. For now, though, we would like to acknowledge this influence in our understanding of the benefits of "being" in centering prayer, which can extend to daily living.

REFERENCES

Burton-Christie, D. (1993). *The Word in the Desert: Scripture and the Quest for Holiness in Early Christian Monasticism.* New York: Oxford University Press.

Chryssavgis, J. (2008). *In the Heart of the Desert: The Spirituality of the Desert Fathers and Mothers.* Bloomington, IN: World Wisdom, Inc.

Finley, J. (2004). *Christian Meditation: Experiencing the Presence of God.* New York: HarperCollins Publishers.

Foster, R. (2011). *Sanctuary of the Soul: Journey into Meditative Prayer.* Downers Grove, IL: InterVarsity Press.

Frenette, D. (2012). *The Path of Centering Prayer: Deepening your Experience of God.* Boulder, CO: Sounds True, Inc.

Gorman, M. (2009). *Inhabiting the Cruciform God: Kenosis, Justification, and Theosis in Paul's Narrative Soteriology.* Grand Rapids, MI: William B. Eerdman's Publishing.

Keating, T. (2006). *The Method of Centering Prayer: The Prayer of Consent.* Butler, NJ: Contemplative Outreach, Ltd.

Keating, T. (2014). *Intimacy with God: An Introduction to Centering Prayer.* New York: Crossroad.

Kostenberger, A. (2009). *A Theology of John's Gospel and Letters.* Grand Rapids, MI: Zondervan.

Nouwen, H. (1981). *Making All Things New: An Invitation to the Spiritual Life.* San Francisco, CA: HarperSanFrancisco.

Segal, Z., Williams, M., & Teasdale, J. (2012). *Mindfulness-Based Cognitive Therapy for Depression* (2nd ed.). New York: The Guilford Press.

WEEK 7

AN INTRODUCTION TO
THE WELCOMING PRAYER

INTRODUCTION

In this chapter, you will learn about the welcoming prayer, which can help you to extend your centering prayer practice to daily life. With the welcoming prayer, you are learning to invite God into your pain, letting go of your own efforts to control the inner world. Instead, you are surrendering to God's sovereignty during moments of distress, which can be especially helpful in your struggle with uncertainty, worry, and anxiety.

Similar to exposure therapy within clinical psychology, the welcoming prayer can assist you in relating differently to your thoughts and feelings, cultivating a compassionate and accepting attitude in the process. What is more, because God is active within your innermost being, you will be learning to allow him to "take the reins," pivoting from your unilateral control efforts to trusting in his divine plan. Along the way, we are hopeful that this practice can help you *pragmatically* with your uncertainty and worry, given that you are not pursuing "approach" or "avoidance" strategies to somehow generate a certain future, as well as *spiritually*, since you will be asking God to be with you in your pain.

To help you better understand the importance of simply "being" with God in the midst of pain, we will be reviewing the story of Mary and Martha in Luke's gospel, exploring the overlap between Mary's yielding posture and the "being" mode in mindfulness-based cognitive therapy (MBCT). To sit at Jesus' feet, from our perspective, means you are in no way trying to generate a different outcome. Rather, you are learning to gaze upon God, recognizing that the most important part of your current experience is to trust in him. As you increasingly welcome God into your experiences, sitting at his feet from moment to moment, you may find you are able to relate differently to uncertainty and worry.

Throughout this week, you will have the opportunity to practice the welcoming prayer, turning to God as you stumble, trip, and fall in daily living. As you get into the habit of formally practicing every day, we are hopeful that your willingness to invite God into your experience of pain, rather than unilaterally trying to make it go away, will help you find rest in him. Above all else, we propose that the greatest strength of the welcoming prayer is that it can increase your ability to trust in God's infinite wisdom, love, and power. It does so as you continually place your faith in God's active, loving presence. Although the psychological pain you are in—consisting of uncertainty, worry, doubt, and anxiety—might not go away, maintaining an awareness of God's presence can help you to endure more effectively. After all, God's grace is more than enough, given we are often a vehicle for his power when we are feeling weak, vulnerable, or frail (1 Corinthians 12:9).

A Brief Overview of the Welcoming Prayer[1]

The welcoming prayer was developed as a way to continue the practice of centering prayer, yielding to God's active, loving presence in the midst of inner pain throughout the day (Bourgeault, 2004). With the practice, we are learning to let go of our own efforts to gain control over the inner world; instead, we are surrendering to God's sovereignty, recognizing that he is infinitely wise and loving when it comes to the difficult thoughts and feelings we may face from moment to moment. If God is all-knowing, all-loving, and all-powerful, relinquishing the grip we have on our inner world can help us to find rest, given that the use of "approach" or "avoidance" strategies to attain certainty has likely failed to deliver lasting results. In other words, God as our creator is sovereign over both our external and internal experiences. Trusting that God accepts us as we are, knows us more intimately than we know ourselves, and is working for us allows us to trust him in the midst of our uncertainty and worry.

To be open to God's loving presence, even in the midst of pain, means we can move in the direction of living the life we want. This reality is in contrast to getting repeatedly sidetracked by worrying thoughts and anxious feelings that might never fully go away. Consistent with centering prayer, we believe the welcoming prayer can help you to further develop this attitude of surrender, putting your faith in God's plan for your inner world. Although you might not be able to fully control whether or not you experience worrying thoughts or anxious feelings from minute to minute and day to day, you *do* have the ability to hand them over to God, asking him to do what he will with them. To be sure, instead of struggling with them, assuming they are "bad" and need to "go away," you are cultivating an attitude of trust. You are stating to God: "I have faith that you have a plan for my thoughts and feelings. Do with them as you wish. I trust you."

Further, these internal experiences are important to God. Because God cares for us, we trust that God is purposeful in our inner struggles. That is, God is facilitating our becoming more like Christ as he remains with us in our uncertainty. As we are reminded in 2 Corinthians 3:18, "And we all, who with unveiled faces contemplate the Lord's glory, are being transformed into his image with ever-increasing glory, which comes from the Lord, who is the Spirit." We are reminded that, through contemplation, we open ourselves more and more to God, who transforms us more closely to be like his Son, Jesus.

In the process, we believe that you are learning to further trust in God's providence, extending this attitude of surrender to your inner world, something that many Christians struggle to do. To deepen your ability to "let go," from our perspective, allows you to find peace in the midst of the storm. You are recognizing that the most important part of your pain is that God is with you. Rather than attempting to control, hold onto, or push away inner events, you are working towards seeing the inner world for what it actually is—impermanent thoughts and feelings. In fact, you can repeatedly give your distress to God as a faithful, trusting gesture, letting him know over and over again that you are allowing him to reside within your innermost being.

One of the most vivid reminders of God being "with us" in times of stress occurs when individuals have encounters with heavenly beings. For example, Mary received an angelic visitor and heard the message, "Do not be afraid, Mary; you have found favor with God" (Luke 1:30). In fact, all the angelic visitations regarding the announcement of Jesus' birth began with "Do not be afraid." This emphasizes that: (a) God recognizes some situations are scary; and (b) we may trust that God has our best interests at heart and is working for our good. Notice that the message to Mary is *not*, "You should not be afraid, your fear and worry are bad or wrong." The message is that God is with us and cares for us in uncertain times.

Recall from several chapters ago that St. Claude de la Colombière's (1980) *Trustful Surrender to Divine Providence*, written sometime around the 1600s, outlined a psychospiritual approach to finding "peace and happiness" in the midst of a variety of painful life events. To surrender to God's plan, from this viewpoint, means that you are no longer questioning the utility of inner pain. Instead, as you notice that you are worrying about an unknown future, experiencing the bodily sensation of anxiety in the process, handing over these distressing psychological events to God can help you fortify your trust in his will. To "drink the cup" that God offers (Luke 22:42), therefore, is about welcoming these inner trials, especially recurrent experiences, when they will not go away. In thinking about how we drink this cup, we need to fully embrace it—acknowledging what is actually in the cup as we gently and intentionally hold it in our hands. That is, we need to recognize the times when we experience stress and worry. Further, we faithfully accept these experiences—this is *my* cup—and do not avoid them. In fact, we purposefully recognize God's active presence while drinking our God-given cup. Although worry and anxiety can be chronic, turning to God in the midst of your suffering can help you recognize that he is with you, guiding the way and orchestrating a plan that has your best intentions in mind (see, for example, Matthew 7:9–11).

Worth mentioning, however, is that God's plan may not always be synonymous with "happiness" or "pleasure." Rather, through the welcoming prayer, you are learning to find God in your pain, recognizing that he may be calling to you in the midst of an inner trial. As C. S. Lewis famously stated, "God whispers to us in our pleasures, speaks in our conscience, but shouts in our pains: it is His megaphone to rouse a deaf world" (quoted in Kilby, 1964, p. 68).

In the context of this eight-week program, the inner distress you experience when you are uncertain can most certainly be viewed as a signal, which tells you that you need to trust in God's divine plan. You are following his steps as he carves out a path for you along the roads of life. Stated differently, instead of viewing uncertainty, worry, and anxiety as "bad" experiences that you need to get rid of through unilateral "approach" and "avoidance" strategies, this type of inner distress can help you to shift towards God's providence, trusting in him because he is infinitely wise, loving, and powerful. These experiences provide opportunities to practice surrendering to God during our uncertainty and worry.

Just like having sore muscles after a long race means you need to take a day to rest, uncertainty, worry, and anxiety can help you to recognize the importance of falling into God's arms. Resting in God is especially salient when you have wandered away, reminiscent of the lost son (Luke 15:11–32). As soon as you notice you are worrying, the welcoming prayer can help you to embrace these inner experiences, given that you are inviting God into the distress. You are trusting that he is present. Because he is with you, there is no need to do anything, other than allow him to work within your inner world.

If you recall our definition of Christian worry, noted again below, you may find that this recurrent, distressing inner experience can serve as a signal to help you turn around. You are shifting from heading down your *own* path to the road *God* has called you to walk with him on, ameliorating the central features of Christian worry in the process:

> The unsuccessful human attempt, through cognitive efforts, to obtain certainty about an ambiguous future because of the struggle to believe in, trust, and surrender to the perfect care of an infinitely wise, loving, and powerful God.

Here, notice that worrying signifies that we are striving, unilaterally, to generate absolute certainty, especially when we are faced with an unknown future. This is *our* path—finding certainty in our efforts to control an uncertain future. Yet, as soon as we recognize we are worrying—as well as experiencing a variety of other anxiety-related symptoms—we can convert this experience into a trustful act of surrender to God's sovereignty. This is *God's* path. God is in control; God knows what we need; God cares deeply for our well-being.

As you reflect on the days, weeks, and months ahead, try to consider what life might be like if you were to view uncertainty, worry, and anxiety as signals that tell you to trust in God's providence. In other words, rather than battling with these inner events, attempting to make them go away through "approach" or "avoidance" strategies, what might life be like if you interpret your inner pain as a way for God to get your attention? What if your distress actually draws you closer to him each time you venture out on your own to control, plan, and predict your future without him? Although by no means easy to do, by interpreting your inner distress as a part of God's plan, we believe you will be more likely to see God in all things. You may be able to recognize that he is active, moving, and loving you from moment to moment. Worded differently, God is with you in your pain, ministering to you and patiently walking alongside you as you struggle with uncertainty and worry.

One of the most beautiful Psalms that focuses on both the experience of inner distress and blessings from God is Psalm 51. This Psalm begins with a cry for God's mercy because of our struggles. The Psalmist begs for God's grace and cleansing so that his relationship with God may be restored. In Psalm 51:17, we read: "My sacrifice, O God, is a broken spirit; a broken and contrite heart you, God, will not despise." In other words, our brokenness reminds us of God's mercy, grace, and care for who we are and our relationship with him.

The Main Ingredients of the Welcoming Prayer

With the welcoming prayer, there are several main ingredients that can help you in your daily struggle with uncertainty, worry, and anxiety. Based on the three main steps—(a) connecting to your inner experience; (b) embracing your inner experience by inviting God into the process; and (c) letting go of futile attempts to control or push away your inner experience because God is sovereign and providentially providing for you (Contemplative Outreach, n.d.)—several characteristics of the practice may help you in the midst of your uncertainty and worry, turning to God in your moment of need:

- The welcoming prayer can help you to get to know your uncertainty, worry, and anxiety, given that you are leaning into the experience, rather than trying to avoid it or push it away. By embracing difficult thoughts and feelings, you are able to live the life God has called you to live, instead of simply reacting to uncertainty, worry, doubt, and anxiety. The welcoming prayer helps us know our inner experience. We begin to hold our inner experience, instead of avoiding or controlling it.
- The welcoming prayer can help you to acknowledge God's presence in the midst of your pain, ministering to you and walking alongside you as you struggle in the present moment, rather than viewing him as distant and uninterested in your suffering. We learn to see God in the midst of our inner struggles. We learn to identify glimpses of God's grace in challenging personal experiences.
- The welcoming prayer can help you to extend centering prayer to daily living, especially your thoughts and feelings, since you are surrendering your inner world to his providential care. Over time, the welcoming prayer can help you to cultivate a deeper trust in God's actions, which extend to inner events, such as distressing thoughts and painful feelings.

Facing Uncertainty and Yielding to God's Presence:
A Two-Pronged Strategy for Worry

In our view, the most important part of the welcoming prayer is its emphasis on turning towards your inner pain, rather than trying to avoid it, coupled with the ability to invite God into the process. To begin, mental health professionals have known for quite some time that one of the best ways to ameliorate anxiety-related symptoms is to actually face them, instead of trying to get rid of them through avoidance strategies that tend to impair daily living. For example, the American Psychological Association's (APA) Society of Clinical Psychology succinctly defines exposure therapy, an evidence-based form of psychotherapy used with a variety of anxiety disorders, as follows:

> In this form of therapy, psychologists create a safe environment in which to "expose" individuals to the things they fear and avoid. The exposure to the feared objects, activities, or situations in a safe environment helps reduce fear and decrease avoidance. (APA, n.d.)

Among other benefits, exposure therapy can help you in the following ways (adapted from APA, n.d.):

- Exposure therapy can help you get used to the fear, given that you are repeatedly exposed to it, recognizing that the feared object, event, or relationship is much less likely to harm you.
- Exposure therapy can assist you in being able to face distressing inner experiences with a sense of confidence and courage, rather than using avoidance, which can make life worse because daily living is impaired.
- Exposure therapy can help you regulate your emotions, including fear and anxiety, in a new way, often with more compassion and less judgment.

Notice that exposure therapy is frequently used to help clients face some of the situations, relationships, or objects they are most afraid of, given that their fears often lead to impairment in functioning due to the seriousness of their avoidance behaviors. Yet, exposure can also be applied to the inner world in order to relate differently to inner distress, since attempts to avoid uncertainty, worry, and anxiety can also lead to an unmanageable life. In other words, our futile attempts to control our inner experience by avoiding certain "unpleasant" thoughts and feelings also lead to distress—we may actually feel worse, and have difficulties in a social, occupational, or other context.

Therefore, with the welcoming prayer, our hope is that you are able to welcome the uncertain, worrying thoughts and anxious feelings that you are attempting to avoid. By welcoming them, you are learning that they do not need to dictate what happens next in your life. You are no longer attempting to attain certainty through "approach" or "avoidance" strategies. Rather, you can focus on what matters most by recognizing that God is with you, letting go of your unhelpful efforts to predict the future along the way.

In addition to getting used to distressing inner experiences, and thus ameliorating the tendency to avoid them, the welcoming prayer can also help you to invite God into the experience. You are asking for him to extend his grace to you in your current suffering. Because God's grace is enough, and because he often displays his power in the midst of human frailty (2 Corinthians 12:9), surrendering to him can help you to attain both psychological and spiritual benefits. This understanding is found in the Apostle Paul's second letter to the Corinthians (12:9–10):

> I will boast all the more gladly about my weaknesses, so that Christ's power may rest on me. That is why, for Christ's sake, I delight in weaknesses, in insults, in hardships, in persecutions, in difficulties. For when I am weak, then I am strong.

Overall, with the welcoming prayer, you are learning to accept the reality of difficult inner experiences (e.g., uncertainty, worry, doubt, anxiety) and develop an inner strength to overcome your inner trials. You are also inviting God into the process, recognizing that he will strengthen you in the midst of your vulnerabilities. The welcoming prayer acknowledges that you will have challenging experiences; yet, you can be open to them because God cares for you and has your best interests at heart, especially during times of stress. Therefore, when you are uncertain and worried, surrendering to him by asking for his grace can, paradoxically, strengthen you as you push forward along the roads of life.

The Story of Mary and Martha and "Being" and "Doing"[2]

Another way to make sense of the benefits of an attitude of surrender, cultivated with the welcoming prayer, comes from the story of Mary and Martha in Luke's gospel (10:38–42):

> As Jesus and his disciples were on their way, he came to a village where a woman named Martha opened her home to him. She had a sister called Mary, who sat at the Lord's feet listening to what he said. But Martha was distracted by all the preparations that had to be made. She came to him and asked, "Lord, don't you care that my sister has left me to do the work by myself? Tell her to help me!" "Martha, Martha," the Lord answered, "you are worried and upset about many things, but few things are needed—or indeed only one. Mary has chosen what is better, and it will not be taken away from her."

In this famous passage, Mary simply sat at Jesus' feet, apparently focused on "being" with Jesus. On the other hand, Martha was preoccupied with "doing," anxiously distracted with a to-do list that was not getting done.

Interestingly, this contrast between "being" and "doing" has also been explored in the context of a mindfulness-based therapy for depression—MBCT (Segal et al., 2012). Within MBCT, the "doing mode" involves constantly trying to fix, problem solve, improve, and so on (Segal et al., 2012). Of course, this "fix it" mentality can be highly effective when we are approaching a given task in our environment. Notice that the doing mode is not "bad." We are often called to complete tasks in life, and a mild level of stress sometimes energizes us to complete these activities. Martha's approach to life is not wrong. We need to clean, make dinner, complete our job, serve in our local church, and fulfill our obligations.

Yet, the "doing mode" is seldom effective when it comes to thoughts and feelings, especially since many of our most distressing inner events will not simply go away. In other words, just because we try to control our thoughts, or avoid our feelings, it does not mean we will somehow attain a permanent state of pleasure and happiness. As another consequence, the "doing mode" often leads to a recurrent struggle with staying rooted in the present moment, since we are warring with our thoughts (which are often focused on the past or future), trying to get them to go away. Above all else, this "doing" approach seems to resemble Martha's anxious, distracted activity. That is, the most important thing that needed to be accomplished when Jesus came to visit was being with him, not completing preparations and work.

In your own life, you may be regularly applying this "doing" approach, reminiscent of Martha, to your uncertainty, worry, doubt, and anxiety, likely coming up short in the long run. Although you may find that you have short-term success by sometimes getting rid of your inner distress, you might also notice that you are distracted from life and exhausted from moment to moment because of all the effort you are spending to "do" something about your pain. You might even see this Martha mentality in your efforts to attain certainty, using "approach" strategies to generate a predictable and controllable future within your immediate environment. In other words, approaching all of life's experiences in the way that Martha approached Jesus when he came to visit is ultimately counterproductive in "fixing" pain and dealing with stress and worry.

Conversely, Mary focused on sitting with Jesus, spending time with him because he was in the room. Likely recognizing that his presence was the most important part of her day, Mary seemed to prioritize fellowshipping with him above other activities. Unlike her sister, she was able to sit at his feet in order to learn from him. Consistent with Mary's approach, MBCT authors typically describe the "being mode" as a way of accepting the present moment, rather than trying to fix or get rid of what is in front of us (Segal et al., 2012). To fully embrace the here and now, like Mary, involves taking your hand off the control switch, letting go of the need to achieve some other inner or outer state. Within the inner world, this means relinquishing the tendency to try to control your thoughts and feelings. On the other hand, the "being mode" in the outer world means learning to accept life's events without constantly trying to micromanage them.

To reconcile Mary's approach with both the "being mode" in MBCT and the welcoming prayer means you are learning to sit patiently at Jesus' feet, without trying to attain a certain, predictable, and controllable future. Rather, you are able to prioritize Jesus' presence as the most important part of this moment, letting go of your own efforts to change by surrendering to him. After all, to change your inner world—or the environment you are in, for that matter—means you may end up driven and distracted, like Martha. You might even miss out on the mystery and awe of Jesus' presence in *this* very moment within *this* very room.

Because he is with you now, there is nowhere else you need to be. With your inner world, you can surrender your uncertain, worrying thoughts to Jesus, letting him do with them what he wishes because you are solely focused on sitting at his feet. Rather than being preoccupied with your anxiety, which emanates from anticipating future catastrophes, you are firmly planted in the here and now, recognizing that Jesus is in the room with you. Because he is with you, your job is to simply "be," trusting that his providential care extends to both your inner and outer world within this very minute, hour, day, week, and year.

IMMANUEL: "GOD IS WITH US"

Related to this discussion, within the first chapter of Matthew's gospel (1:22–23), Jesus is described as "Immanuel," or "God with us." Drawing from Isaiah 7:14, the author of Matthew highlighted the salience of Jesus' birth, given that Jesus would eventually "save his people from their sins" (1:21) by dwelling among them and offering himself as a sacrifice on a cross. Therefore, with the incarnation, Jesus came to earth to be *with* humankind. Because Jesus no longer walks with us in physical form, he offers humans in the twenty-first century a "spiritual presence" (France, 2007).

If you can, try to imagine what your life would be like if you truly believed that Jesus is with you, walking alongside you as you experience uncertainty, worry, doubt, and anxiety. Instead of having to deal with these difficult inner events on your own, Jesus knows what human suffering is like, understanding firsthand your struggles and shortcomings (Hebrews 4:15). After all, he experienced all this world has to offer, suffering and dying to reconcile humankind to God. Because of this, the welcoming prayer can help you to further develop the ability to recognize Jesus' presence, given he is with you as you experience both inner pain and stressful life events. Although you may

INSTRUCTIONS FOR THE WELCOMING PRAYER

not be able to predict your future with certainty, acknowledging Jesus' presence can help you to find the strength to endure. This endurance will help you to press forward on the trails of life with Jesus as your traveling companion.

INSTRUCTIONS FOR THE WELCOMING PRAYER

In terms of the actual instructions for the welcoming prayer, this week you will be applying the practice to uncertainty, worry, and anxiety (adapted from Contemplative Outreach, n.d.):

1. "Focus, feel, and sink into" your thoughts of uncertainty and worry and feeling of anxiety. Try to be especially aware of the physiological sensation of anxiety, including where it is located in your body. For example, you may feel tightness in your chest, or a racing heartbeat. Also, see if you can just notice the thoughts that are passing through your mind, without judging them or trying to change them in any way.
2. "Welcome" your uncertain, worrying thoughts, along with your anxious feelings, inviting God into the process and fully surrendering these inner experiences to him. Be open to these uncertain thoughts, and recognize that God is with you—God cares for you, and is especially close in your distress.
3. "Let go" of your efforts to control or manage your thoughts and feelings, including worry and anxiety. Also, "let go" of your desire to control, manage, and predict an unknown future on your own, trusting in God's providence to illuminate your future paths. Truly imagine relinquishing your grip, handing to God your efforts at control and putting your faith in his sovereign, benevolent care.

EXERCISE: THE 20-MINUTE WELCOMING PRAYER MEDITATION

Find a quiet environment, sitting upright in a comfortable chair with your feet on the ground and hands resting in your lap. When you are ready, begin to listen to the audio version of the welcoming prayer (Track 5 at https://www.routledge.com/Contemplative-Prayer-for-Christians-with-Chronic-Worry-An-Eight-Week-Program/Knabb-Frederick/p/book/9781138690943 under the eResource tab). Or, you can follow along with the transcript below (adapted from Contemplative Outreach, n.d.):

- Begin by closing your eyes, asking Jesus to be with you as you begin this formal practice. Now, start to notice your thoughts about uncertainty, recognizing that you are anticipating future catastrophe. Acknowledge that they are just thoughts. Allow them to run their natural course as you maintain an attitude of non-judgment and compassion. As if you are seeing them for the first time, try to notice them with a sense of mystery and awe. Just focus on gently embracing them, rather than trying to tightly clutch them or get rid of them.
- Next, see if you can welcome them, moving beyond merely noticing them. Actually try to embrace them, inviting God into the process. In other words, ask God to be with you in the midst of your uncertain, worrying thoughts. See if you can just give them to God, since he is with you as you engage in this practice. Again, invite God to be with you in the midst of your uncertainties and worries, recognizing that he will do with them what he pleases.
- After you have invited him into your thinking process, "let go" of the tendency to use worry to generate certainty, noticing your thoughts with a sense of peace because God is with you. Reminiscent of Mary sitting at Jesus' feet, just focus on God's presence, allowing Jesus to do

what he wants to do in this moment. Rather than trying to "fix" your thoughts, consistent with Martha's "doing," just "be" with Jesus as your mind generates thoughts. Relinquish the need to change the thoughts you are having. Each time a thought comes up, whether it relates to worry or another distracting inner event, just hand it over to Jesus. Surrender to him in the process.

- As a next step, see if you can connect with your bodily experience of anxiety, noticing where you are feeling anxious. You may have tightness in your chest, rapid heartbeat, or sweaty palms. As you notice these anxiety-related experiences, see if you can just be with them, inviting Jesus into the process. Instead of labeling your anxiety as somehow "bad," try to just focus on Jesus' presence, recognizing that he is in control.

- Now, "let go" of your tendency to control your anxiety, surrendering to Jesus as you sit patiently at his feet. In fact, see if you can embrace your anxiety, given you are trusting that Jesus will do with it what he wishes. If he would like for it to stay, it will stay. Your job, in this moment, is to fully accept your inner world, based on the notion that you are sitting at Jesus' feet. You are solely focused on "being." Fully relinquish your need to change your uncertain, worrying thoughts and anxiety-related feelings. Instead, just surrender to Jesus, recognizing that he is sovereign over your inner world.

- Moreover, "let go" of your need to control, manage, and predict the future, trusting in Jesus' providence in this very moment. In other words, rather than looking to the future, just sit with him, recognizing that he will carve out the best path for you—today, tomorrow, next week, and next year. Because he is infinitely wise, loving, and powerful, he already knows what will happen next, and is helping you to continue to grow in your relationship with him. Trusting in him, see if you can just enjoy sitting at his feet, basking in the freedom you have because you have transferred control to him.

- As this practice comes to a close, see if you can extend your ability to surrender your inner world to God to daily living. Throughout your day, see if you can briefly "embrace," "welcome," and "let go" when you notice you are experiencing uncertain, worrying thoughts and anxious feelings. Recognize that God is with you, and is illuminating your paths from moment to moment.

Exercise: Recording Your Daily Efforts for the Welcoming Prayer

In the space that follows, see if you can briefly document your daily experience of the welcoming prayer (beyond what you have documented in the space above).

Day of the Week	Length of Time Practiced (Minutes)	Experience of Uncertainty, Doubt, Worry, and Anxiety Before and After the Exercise	Experience of God's Active, Loving Presence Before and After the Exercise	Inner Barriers to the Welcoming Prayer (Thoughts, Feelings, and Sensations)	Outer Barriers to the Welcoming Prayer (Distractions in the Environment)
Monday					
Tuesday					

Wednesday					
Thursday					
Friday					
Saturday					
Sunday					

Exercise: Journaling about Your Experience of the Welcoming Prayer

In the space below, try to journal about your experience of the welcoming prayer on a daily basis (beyond what you have documented in the space above). You may wish to explore your relationship with God, as well as your inner experience of uncertainty, doubt, worry, and anxiety before and after the practice.

Monday

Tuesday

Wednesday

Thursday

An Introduction to the Welcoming Prayer

Friday

Saturday

Sunday

Exercise: Homework for the Week

1. Practice the above 20-minute welcoming prayer exercise at least once per day for the entire week. Document these experiences in the space provided above.
2. Journal for at least 10 minutes per day about the welcoming prayer exercise (in the space provided above), focusing on what the experience was like and any potential barriers (e.g., thoughts, feelings, sensations).

Welcoming Jesus into Uncertainty and Doubt: The Experience of Erin, Ryan, and Lisa

For Erin, the seventh week helped her to recognize that Jesus was with her, even when she felt anxious and uncertain about the future. Although she felt isolated and alone in childhood, the welcoming prayer allowed her to find Jesus in the midst of her struggles, ameliorating the tendency to unilaterally attempt to control her future. As she welcomed Jesus into her inner distress, letting go of the tendency to try to fix or manage her pain on her own, she experienced a tremendous sense of peace.

Of course, the pain did not go away; yet, asking Jesus to be with her helped her to endure, continuing on because she had him as a trustworthy, loving travel companion. Through daily practice, she discovered that Jesus had always been there, helping her through her parents' divorce and comforting her in the midst of her inner and outer trials. By relinquishing the grip that she attempted to maintain on an unknown future, turning to Jesus in the process, she was able to go about her day. She was also able to find comfort in even the most difficult situations.

Ryan's experience of the seventh week of the program was similar to Erin's experience. As he repeatedly invited Jesus into his pain, he found that he was able to relate to it in a new way, embracing his uncertainty and worry because God was dwelling with him. Rather than questioning if God was there, assuming God was absent because he was hurting, Ryan continued to trust that Jesus was moving in his life.

In daily living, Ryan noticed that he was more effective when it came to making decisions, given he was much more aware of Jesus' presence. Based on his awareness of God's powerful, loving presence, Ryan was increasingly able to place his faith in God's infinite wisdom to illuminate his paths. Instead of being preoccupied with surprises, based in part on an unexpected breakup in college, Ryan felt more confident in his ability to "let go." He was able to surrender to God's providence because he was no longer trying to eliminate his pain. Using his uncertainty and worry as a signal, Ryan repeatedly invited God into his pain throughout his day, which helped him to accept his inner distress and deepen his faith in God as all-knowing, all-loving, and all-powerful.

With Lisa, the welcoming prayer was most helpful in allowing her to surrender her inner struggles to God, letting go of the tendency to want to "make the pain go away" through worrying and compulsively checking. As she practiced welcoming her uncertainty, worry, doubt, and anxiety, she noticed that these inner experiences were just that—passing events that were in no way permanent.

What is more, because God was with her in the midst of these inner trials, she became increasingly confident that she could endure, trusting in God to carve out the best path for her life.

Ultimately, in their own ways, Erin, Ryan, and Lisa were all able to continue to deepen their ability to trust in God, using formal practice to help them extend this newfound psychological and spiritual awareness to daily living. Although each of them continued to experience uncertainty, worry, and anxiety, they found that God's presence helped them to continue on, finding peace in the midst of the storm because Immanuel was there. To reiterate, the welcoming prayer by no means led to the complete eradication of their inner distress; still, formal practice helped Erin, Ryan, and Lisa to relate differently to their pain, finding comfort in Jesus' understanding of their struggles.

Conclusion

In the seventh week of the program, you learned about the welcoming prayer, which can help you continue to develop the ability to surrender to God's providential care. As you applied this attitude of surrender to your inner pain, our hope is that you were able to relate differently to your worry and anxiety, accepting the uncertainties of life because the alternative—avoidance—simply has not worked in the past. Rather, inviting Jesus (i.e., Immanuel) into the pain can help you to deepen your trust in him. Over time, you are better able to recognize that he is active, present, and working even in the most challenging of situations.

Above all else, each of the contemplative practices in this program have been offered to allow you to yield to God's active, loving presence, given that he is all-knowing, all-loving, and all-powerful. These attributes mean you can trust in his guidance for your life. In the context of uncertainty, worry, and anxiety, these inner experiences may never fully go away; yet, by inviting God into the process, we believe you are preparing yourself to more effectively deal with the pains of daily living. Because the future is unknown, surrendering your inner and outer world to God can help you be present to what is unfolding around you, rather than getting sidetracked in your efforts to attain certainty.

In the last week of the program, you will have the opportunity to solidify your gains, reflecting on the different contemplative exercises you have practiced and exploring the ways in which you have learned to relate differently to your uncertainty, worry, and anxiety. Our hope is that you will continue on with daily contemplative practice, which can help you to apply an attitude of trustful surrender to all of life. Instead of striving to predict and control your own future, outside of God's design, trusting in God's benevolent care can help you to find peace in all situations (Philippians 4:11–13).

Notes

1 For a more detailed review of the central ingredients of the welcoming prayer (developed by Mary Mrozowski), see Bourgeault (2004) and Haisten (2005). Currently, Contemplative Outreach (www.contemplativeoutreach.org) offers a range of workshops and trainings on the practice.

2 For a more detailed summary of the overlap between the welcoming prayer and the story of Mary and Martha in Luke's gospel, see Haisten (2005). Over the years, a plethora of contemplative writers (see Butler, 2003) have pointed to Mary's yielding posture to illuminate a life of contemplation, whereas Martha's activity represents a life of action, service, and self-sacrifice. Consistent with this interpretation, Haisten advocated for the importance of Mary's yielding attitude of surrender, captured in the modern contemplative practice of the welcoming prayer. Moreover, in this short writing, Haisten discussed the welcoming prayer in the context of surrendering to God's providential care. Although she drew from Caussade's (2011) *Abandonment to Divine Providence*, rather than St. Claude de la Colombière's (1980) *Trustful Surrender to Divine Providence*, both centuries-old Jesuit works are considered timeless spiritual classics. In fact, both advocate for the importance of daily surrender to God in order to find peace in the midst of suffering.

REFERENCES

American Psychological Association (APA) (n.d.). *What is Exposure Therapy?* Retrieved April 20, 2016 from www.div12.org/sites/default/files/WhatIsExposureTherapy.pdf

Bourgeault, C. (2004). *Centering Prayer and Inner Awakening.* New York: Cowley Publications.

Butler, D. (2003). *Western Mysticism: Augustine, Gregory and Bernard on Contemplation and the Contemplative Life.* Mineola, NY: Dover Publications, Inc.

Caussade, J. (2011). *Abandonment to Divine Providence.* San Francisco: Ignatius Press.

Contemplative Outreach. (n.d.). *The Welcoming Prayer.* Retrieved April 20, 2016 from www.contemplativeoutreach.org

France, R. (2007). *The Gospel of Matthew.* Grand Rapids, MI: William B. Eerdmans Publishing Company.

Haisten, C. (2005). *The Practice of Welcoming Prayer.* Butler, NJ: Contemplative Outreach, Ltd.

Kilby, C. (1964). *The Christian World of C. S. Lewis.* Grand Rapids, MI: William B. Eerdmans Publishing Company.

Segal, Z., Williams, M., & Teasdale, J. (2012). *Mindfulness-Based Cognitive Therapy for Depression* (2nd ed.). New York: The Guilford Press.

St. Claude de la Colombière. (1980). *Trustful Surrender to Divine Providence: The Secret of Peace and Happiness.* Charlotte, NC: Tan Books.

Week 8

SURRENDERING TO DIVINE PROVIDENCE IN DAILY LIVING

Introduction

In the last week of the program, you will review the importance of surrendering to God's providence, as well as re-examine contemplative prayer as a vehicle through which you can cultivate an attitude of surrender in the presence of God. You will also briefly explore the benefits of surrendering in daily living, extending your formal practice to day-to-day experiences. Relatedly, you will have the opportunity to look out into the future, planning for a lifetime of letting go in order to place your faith in God's infinite wisdom, love, and power when you notice you are uncertain, worrying, and anxious.

We will also introduce one final exercise—a brief breathing activity to help you turn from "doing" to "being" (Segal et al., 2012) in the real world. You will also have the opportunity to identify several passages in scripture that focus on surrendering to God, which can encourage you as you steadily travel down the roads of life. To conclude the program, we will check in with Erin, Ryan, and Lisa one last time in order to observe the changes they have experienced along the way.

A Review of Surrendering to God's Providence

In this eight-week program, you have worked on cultivating a deeper sense of God's providential care, focusing on his infinite wisdom, goodness, and power. Rooted in scripture, we believe these attributes can help you to let go of the tendency to use "approach" or "avoidance" strategies to attain a pseudo-sense of certainty about an unknown future. Rather than unilaterally striving to generate predictability and control, falling into God's arms from moment to moment can help you live the life you truly want, anchored to a deeper, more trusting relationship with him.

In fact, this idea of trustful surrender is exemplified beautifully in the biblical story of Esther, who stood with her people in Babylonian exile.[1] The entire story is connected with a deep sense of God's abiding care and Esther's trustful surrender to being placed in a challenging situation. Recall that Esther was actually adopted by Mordecai. This is an important fact, as King Xerxes needed to replace his former queen, Vashti, because she fell short of his expectations. In order to find a new queen, King Xerxes decided to recruit women throughout his kingdom to join his harem. After 12 months of living in the harem, Esther was selected to be the new queen. During the entire time Esther was living in the harem, Mordecai was there, walking by the windows so he could see what

117

was happening to her. He was concerned because he instructed Esther to keep her Jewish heritage a secret. Mordecai learned of a plot by two guards to kill the king, so he warned Esther, who warned the king. This resulted in Mordecai receiving official recognition by the king.

Next, we are introduced to Haman. Haman was a proud individual, exalted to be the second person in the entire kingdom. Haman had King Xerxes declare that everyone should bow to him whenever he was seen. Mordecai declined, and Haman convinced the king to make a declaration to kill Mordecai and all his family, even his entire race. Mordecai turned to Esther to talk with the king. However, Esther could not approach the king without being summoned, given that doing so would mean death. Esther had to trust that God placed her in that situation to be an instrument of salvation for her people. Certainly, Esther had to trust that by surrendering to God's call to approach the king, she would be saved and spared.

Over time, we believe this attitude of surrender can help you in your most important relationships, work life, church life, and so on, given that you are learning to trust in God's will. This deep trust is reminiscent of Jesus in the gospels. To regularly yield to God's authority, in turn, is pleasing to him (see Matthew 25:14–23): "Well done, good and faithful servant!" To faithfully serve the master, certainly, is beneficial to *both* the servant *and* the master.

CONTEMPLATION AS A VEHICLE FOR SURRENDERING

On a daily basis, you have been able to practice this attitude of surrender through contemplative practice. Our hope is that you have moved in the direction of yielding to God's will in both the inner and outer world. With your thoughts, feelings, and sensations, contemplative practice can help you offer your innermost being to God, trusting in him to heal you in the process. Of course, healing is not necessarily synonymous with making difficult thoughts, feelings, and sensations go away. Rather, healing involves finding peace in the reality that God is with you in the midst of your uncertainty, worry, doubt, and anxiety. He is walking alongside you as you struggle from moment to moment. Remember Jesus' words: "My Father, if it is possible, may this cup be taken from me. Yet not as I will, but as you will" (Matthew 26:39). God is with us in our uncertain times and experiences.

With the outer world, our hope is that daily contemplative practice has helped you to "transfer the reins" to God, recognizing that the unknown future you face is in his proverbial hands. Instead of striving, on your own, to generate a pseudo-certain future (which is not possible), we believe contemplative prayer can help you to gain a greater awareness of God's infinite wisdom, love, and power. You are deepening your trust in him, leaning on him to guide you along the roads of life. These contemplative practices, we hope, have allowed you to experience God being "with you"—God is with you in your inner struggles with anxiety, worry, and stress. Imagine that life is an extended road trip. Many of the paths you drive on will lack proper lighting, and consist of potholes, cracks, and so on. Yet, because God is your driver, you are able to shut your eyes from time to time to get much-needed rest, since God will safely guide you to your destination.

THE BENEFITS OF SURRENDER IN DAILY LIFE

In your efforts to practice contemplative prayer on a daily basis, we are hopeful you have started to see that the seeds you have planted are sprouting in everyday life. To walk through this world with a gentler, kinder attitude can definitely help you in your ability to let go of your need to create absolute certainty. Instead, you are able to enjoy God's gift to you—life itself.

As you wake up each day, contemplative prayer can prepare you for an unknown, uncertain future, given that you are saying to God, "Your kingdom come, your will be done, on earth as it is in heaven" (Matthew 6:10). In turn, as you walk out your front door to start your day, you may find that you have an added confidence when facing daily events because you firmly trust that God's will is best for your life. In that God knows all of the possible roads you can take, and because he is all-loving and all-powerful, he is able to guide you towards the best possible destination. He is even sanctifying you along the way.

Looking Forward: Surrender as a Lifelong Pursuit

Beyond applying contemplative prayer to daily life, our desire is for you to extend the practice to the months, years, and decades that lie ahead. Rather than viewing contemplative prayer as a means to an end (ameliorating uncertainty, worry, doubt, and anxiety), our hope is that you will view the practice as a way to finish the race strong (2 Timothy 4:7), living a long life devoted to yielding to God's will from moment to moment. Reminiscent of Jesus' mission to radically pursue his Father's will while on this planet (John 6:38), we believe that healthy psychological and spiritual functioning in the Christian life involves aligning our will with the will of our maker, designer, and Lord.

The parable of the vine and branches is especially instructive here. John 15:1–4 reads as follows:

> I am the true vine, and my Father is the gardener. He cuts off every branch in me that bears no fruit, while every branch that does bear fruit he prunes so that it will be even more fruitful. You are already clean because of the word I have spoken to you. Remain in me, as I also remain in you. No branch can bear fruit by itself; it must remain in the vine. Neither can you bear fruit unless you remain in me.

With contemplative practice, the idea is that it takes a lifetime. As Jesus reminded us, he is the true vine, and we branch off from him. We must trust in the vine's nourishment and support in order to grow. Further, we must surrender to the care of the gardener in order to increase our fruitfulness. We must trust in the methods—i.e., contemplative practice—to increase our Christlikeness, i.e., fruitfulness. As indicated in John 15, we will inevitably need pruning. That is, God is with us in our difficult experiences, and these experiences have a purpose—to increase our Christlikeness.

Across the lifespan, our hope is that you will see surrender as a process (rather than a fixed, static outcome), given that you will continue to work on it from moment to moment, day to day, and year to year. In other words, this ongoing process of yielding to God's will involves asking the following question: "How, in this very moment, can I surrender my inner and outer world to God's plan, trusting in his providential care?"

In turn, effective problem solving involves: (a) discerning God's will, captured by way of personally studying scripture; (b) consistently hearing the preaching of God's word; (c) relying on mature Christian relationships for wisdom; (d) participation in the sacraments of communion and baptism; and (e) prayerful reflection. Stated differently, solving problems with God-given wisdom consists of turning to him, instead of employing worry to "fill in the blanks," in isolation from God. This problem, to be sure, has existed since the third chapter of Genesis, when Adam and Eve ate from the *tree of the knowledge of good and evil*, striving to be like God, rather than radically dependent on him for truth (see Bonhoeffer, 1959).

"It Is Well with My Soul": The Hymn that Captures
Surrendering to God's Providence

Over a century ago, Horatio Spafford wrote, "It Is Well with My Soul." In this famous hymn, we believe the central tenets of our eight-week program are fully captured, given the song's emphasis is on trusting in God, regardless of life's experiences. Try to slowly read through the hymn below, reflecting on the words. You may even want to purchase an audio version to sing along to on a daily basis, worshipping God in the process.

When peace, like a river, attendeth my way,

When sorrows like sea billows roll;

Whatever my lot, Thou has taught me to say,

It is well, it is well, with my soul.

It is well, with my soul,

It is well, with my soul,

It is well, it is well, with my soul.

Though Satan should buffet, though trials should come,

Let this blest assurance control,

That Christ has regarded my helpless estate,

And hath shed His own blood for my soul.

My sin, oh, the bliss of this glorious thought!

My sin, not in part but the whole,

Is nailed to the cross, and I bear it no more,

Praise the Lord, praise the Lord, O my soul!

For me, be it Christ, be it Christ hence to live:

If Jordan above me shall roll,

No pang shall be mine, for in death as in life

Thou wilt whisper Thy peace to my soul.

But, Lord, 'tis for Thee, for Thy coming we wait,

The sky, not the grave, is our goal;

Oh trump of the angel! Oh voice of the Lord!

Blessèd hope, blessèd rest of my soul!

And Lord, haste the day when my faith shall be sight,

The clouds be rolled back as a scroll;

The trump shall resound, and the Lord shall descend,

Even so, it is well with my soul.

In the space that follows, see if you can journal for a few minutes about your reactions to this song, applying the central tenets to your own struggle with uncertainty, worry, doubt, and anxiety. Questions to consider:

- What are some of the life events that the author referred to?
- What allowed him to state, "It is well with my soul," over and over again?
- What role, if any, did God play in his ability to experience well-being, despite life's circumstances?
- How can you apply this message to your own struggle with uncertainty, cultivating this well-being in the depths of your being?

- What role, if any, can God play in this process, helping you to experience a deeper sense of well-being, regardless of what happens in life?

_____

_____

_____

_____

_____

_____

_____

_____

_____

Breathing with Christ: Cultivating an Attitude of Surrender in the Real World

In the last week of the program, we would like to teach you one last contemplative strategy to help with your uncertainty, worry, and anxiety, extending the practice to moments in the real world that often keep you stuck. Beyond formal practice, you have the ability to surrender to God in each passing moment, captured in your breathing. In other words, because God has given you the "breath of life" (Genesis 2:7), you can easily bring your awareness to the breathing process, anchoring yourself to God's active, loving presence by focusing on your breathing for three minutes at a time.

Consistent with mindfulness-based cognitive therapy's (MBCT) (Segal et al., 2012) "three-minute breathing space," this practice can help you to let go in daily living when you notice you are worrying to generate a predictable, controllable future. For example, on your lunch break at work, you can sit in your parked car and focus on God's providence, captured in the fact that you are breathing. Given that you do not need to control your breathing, you can let go, recognizing that God is offering you the "breath of life" from moment to moment. As you connect to your breathing, you can let go of the tendency to control your thoughts, feelings, and sensations, yielding to God's sovereignty over your inner world as you sit in silence with him. "Breathing in fills us up, and breathing out empties us. Breathing in causes us to hold on, and breathing out causes us to let go" (Talbot, 2013, p. 17). Reminiscent of Mary sitting at Jesus' feet (Luke 10:38–42), you are simply focusing on relinquishing the already tenuous grip you have on both the inner and outer world, putting your trust in his active, loving presence for three-minute blocks of time.

Serving as a condensed version of the breathing practice you learned about in the second week of the program, you may find that this three-minute exercise—breathing with Jesus—can help you to cultivate an attitude of surrender wherever you are throughout your day. Over time, our hope is that this practice can serve as a reminder that Jesus is always with you, offering you "living water" (John 4:14) from moment to moment. Certainly, because God offers you his mercy and grace, your life is in his hands.

If you can, try to simply close your eyes, and imagine that Jesus is with you. As you spend these three minutes with him, try to imagine that Jesus is giving you the "breath of life," controlling your breathing as each second passes by. Your job, therefore, is to simply allow Jesus to be in control, letting go of all your own efforts to control your breathing or manage other inner events (thoughts, feelings, and sensations). In this three-minute period of time, you are just noticing that Jesus is graciously offering you the air that fills your lungs as you let go of the tendency to attain a pseudo-sense of certainty through worry and "approach" and "avoidance" strategies.

Our hope is that you will practice this three-minute exercise at least three times per day, in addition to your formal practice, which can help you surrender to God throughout your busy life. Rather than waiting to practice surrender until you get home from a fast-paced day, try to deepen your ability to surrender via this short exercise. Again, using the contemplative practice from the second chapter as a guide, shorten the practice to include three minutes of sitting with Jesus, trusting that he is guiding both your inner and outer world as he generously offers you the breath of life.

EXERCISE: THREE-MINUTE BREATHING WITH JESUS[2]

In this three-minute exercise, adapted from Finley's (2004) and Segal et al.'s (2012) recommendations, please get into a comfortable position, planning on three minutes of silent, wordless prayer. In this time, you will want to find a comfortable seat in a quiet environment, free from distractions. You can start by listening to the audio file that accompanies this book (Track 6 at https://www.routledge.com/Contemplative-Prayer-for-Christians-with-Chronic-Worry-An-Eight-Week-Program/Knabb-Frederick/p/book/9781138690943 under the eResource tab), eventually learning how to enter into this time on your own.

- When you are ready, get into a comfortable position, closing your eyes and saying a brief prayer to God. "Jesus, in the next three minutes, I am surrendering both my inner and outer world to you, letting go of my own efforts to control or predict my future by striving for absolute certainty. Instead, I am giving over my thoughts, feelings, and sensations to you, with my breath serving as a symbol of this yielding, consenting attitude of surrender. I pray that you are with me, guiding this process as I repeatedly surrender to you."
- Now, begin to notice that you are breathing, paying attention to your breath in a specific location throughout the breathing cycle. You might want to focus on the air going in and out of your nostrils, or your abdomen expanding and constricting. In either case, pay close attention to the reality that you do not need to control your breathing in any way. Instead, Jesus is with you, controlling your breath and offering you the "breath of life." As you gently inhale and exhale, let go of your own efforts to control the process, trusting that Jesus is sustaining you by controlling your breathing.
- Continue to sink further and further into this reality, letting go of all your own efforts with each breath. Since Jesus is active and present, there is nothing you need to be doing, other than focusing on Jesus' presence and gift—your breath going in and out of your lungs. Repeatedly, let go of the tendency to want to think or feel a certain way, recognizing that Jesus is completely and totally sovereign. He is loving you and offering you grace and mercy as he interacts with you in a personal, life-giving manner in this very moment.

Surrendering in the Bible: Key Verses to Reflect on During the Day

Below are several Bible verses from the Psalms that emphasize God's attributes, helping you to faithfully surrender to him. If possible, try to memorize some of them (or your own Psalms you have identified) in order to recite them throughout your day. Rather than ruminating about the past or worrying about the future, focus your attention on these passages, meditating on them in order to keep your attention on God during the day:

- "Be still before the Lord and wait patiently for him" (Psalm 37:7).
- "The salvation of the righteous comes from the Lord; he is their stronghold in time of trouble. The Lord helps them and delivers them; he delivers them from the wicked and saves them, because they take refuge in him" (Psalm 37:39–40).
- "When I am afraid, I put my trust in you" (Psalm 56:3).
- "The Lord is trustworthy in all he promises and faithful in all he does. The Lord upholds all who fall and lifts up all who are bowed down" (Psalm 145:13–14).
- "The Lord is righteous in all his ways and faithful in all he does. The Lord is near to all who call on him, to all who call on him in truth. He fulfills the desires of those who fear him; he hears their cry and saves them" (Psalm 145:17–19).

Interestingly, many of the early desert Christians recited the Psalms throughout their day as a way to focus their attention on God. Given that they often faced a wide range of difficult inner experiences in the unpleasant desert terrain—such as painful memories, tempting thoughts, worries about the future, boredom, and so on—they would employ the Psalms as a way to remember God's promises: "Such an approach to Scripture involved saying the words of a particular text, mulling them over in the mind, chewing on and slowly digesting the words" (Burton-Christie, 1993, p. 122).

Unfortunately, we can often get stuck "mulling over" past conversations or memories, as well as "chewing on" worries in order to generate a certain, predictable future. When this happens, our mind is distracted, pulled away from the joy we can experience in union with God. Thus, shifting from ruminating thoughts about the past and worrying thoughts about the future to God's promises in scripture can help you focus on what is praiseworthy, true, and noble (see Philippians 4:8).

In the space below, see if you can identify your own Psalms, which you can recite throughout the day as a way to keep your eyes on God, including his infinite wisdom, love, and power:

1. _____

   _____

2. _____

   _____

3. _____

   _____

4. _____

_____

5. _____

_____

CONCLUDING THE PROGRAM WITH ERIN, RYAN, AND LISA

As Erin, Ryan, and Lisa concluded the program, all three were determined to continue on with daily contemplative practice. In their own way, each of them entered the program preoccupied with uncertainty, influenced by painful, often traumatic life events. Yet, as they settled into the silence and stillness that contemplative practice offers, they were able to slowly let go of their unilateral attempts to generate certainty.

Above all else, their success involved learning to surrender to God, even when they were hurting, uncertain, or stuck, rather than striving to control their inner and outer world. By doing this, Erin, Ryan, and Lisa found that they were more effectively able to make decisions in life, given they were walking with God by their side. Although their worries, doubts, and anxiety did not go away, they were able to relate differently to these inner experiences, given that God's power is perfected in human frailty and vulnerability (2 Corinthians 12:9). In turn, they increasingly turned to scripture, prayer, and Christian relationships to navigate the roads of life.

CONCLUSION

With this program, our hope is that you have been able to improve in your ability to trust in God, given he is all-knowing, all-loving, and all-powerful. Because God is with you, the uncertainties of the future can be tolerated, even accepted with a sense of hope and confidence. Since God is illuminating your paths, walking beside you on the trails of life, the future can be relinquished to him.

When you experience uncertainty, worry, doubt, and anxiety, contemplative practice can help you to "transfer the reins" to God, patiently sitting at Jesus' feet. This new approach to life is in contrast to scurrying about, attempting to micromanage your inner and outer world. With the three-minute breathing exercise, our hope is that you are able to extend your formal practice to daily living, taking breaks to find rest in God, rather than pursuing certainty through ineffective "approach" and "avoidance" strategies. By doing this, we believe you are better prepared to follow Jesus, yielding to God's will in order to drink the perfect cup (Luke 22:42) that he offers you in each and every moment.

By regularly reaching for God, who is *already* with you, we believe you will be better prepared to ameliorate chronic worry, surrendering to God's providential care in the process. This attitude of surrender, certainly, is pleasing to God, given that you are attempting to align your will with his plan for you. As you do this, you have a trustworthy, safe traveling companion, Jesus, who has your best interests in mind:

And surely I am with you always, to the very end of the age. (Matthew 28:20)

Notes

1 The following two paragraphs are summarized from the book of Esther.

2 This is a slightly adapted, three-minute version of the 20-minute exercise in the second week of the program.

References

Bonhoeffer, D. (1959). *Creation and Fall*. New York: Touchstone.

Burton-Christie, D. (1993). *The Word in the Desert: Scripture and the Quest for Holiness in Early Christian Monasticism.* New York: Oxford University Press.

Finley, J. (2004). *Christian Meditation: Experiencing the Presence of God*. New York: HarperCollins Publishers.

Segal, Z., Williams, M., & Teasdale, J. (2012). *Mindfulness-Based Cognitive Therapy for Depression* (2nd ed.). New York: The Guilford Press.

Talbot, J. (2013). *The Jesus Prayer: A Cry for Mercy, a Path of Renewal*. Downers Grove, IL: InterVarsity Press.

INDEX

acceptance 2, 21, 57
Adam and Eve 119
ambiguity *see* uncertainty
American Psychological Association (APA) 106
Anderson, R. 28
anxiety 1, 17, 23; case examples 6–7, 36–37, 52, 68, 86, 114–115, 124; centering prayer 70, 80, 83, 87, 89, 91; daily examen 48–49; distracting thoughts 79; "doing" mode 107; Ignatian prayer 40; Jesus Prayer 53, 54, 56, 60, 66; just "being" 93–94, 108; psychological understanding of worry 2; self-emptying 77; surrender to God 124; uncertainty and 9, 13, 16; welcoming prayer 102, 105, 109, 110, 115
apophatic tradition 24–25, 26, 29, 68, 70, 78, 80, 93
appreciation 47
approach or avoidance strategies 11, 22, 76, 79, 93, 102–103, 104, 108, 117

baptism 119
"being", just 92–94, 101, 102, 107–108, 110
beliefs: about uncertainty 9–11; about worry 15–16
bereavement 7, 68
Bonhoeffer, D. 28
boredom 23, 55, 72, 123
Bourgeault, C. 76–77, 115n1
"breath of life" 31, 57, 121, 122
breathing 31, 117; Jesus Prayer 57, 59, 60, 61; "three-minute breathing with Jesus" 30, 121–122
Buddhism 4
Burton-Christie, D. 123

Caussade, J. 115n2
centering prayer 19, 24, 29, 70–86, 87–101; 20-minute exercise 81–82, 85, 96–97, 100; benefits of the 79–80; case examples 85–86; consenting to God 88–89; "contemplative attitudes" 95–96; detachment 94–95; distracting thoughts 78–79; expectations about the 80–81; false self 72–75; gentler approach to life 90–91; God's loving arms 94; history of the 71; homework 85, 100; instructions for the 81, 96; journaling 83–85, 98–100; just "being" 92–94; *kenosis* 76–77, 86, 95; main tenets 71–72; openness 89; receptivity 77–78; recording your efforts 82, 97; rest 75–76, 91–92; silence 75; simple life 89–90

children 72
christification 27–28
Christlikeness 28, 77, 95, 119
The Cloud of Unknowing 25, 26–27, 70, 71, 72, 78, 86n1
communion 119
compassion 4, 30, 55; exposure therapy 106; Jesus Prayer 53, 56, 59, 60, 61, 68; welcoming prayer 19–20, 109
conformity to divine providence exercise 49–50, 52
Coniaris, A. 27
consent 71, 88–89, 90, 91, 95, 96
contemplation 39, 40, 118
"contemplative attitudes" 87, 95–96, 101
Contemplative Outreach 105, 109, 115n1
contemplative prayer 4, 5, 17–18, 19; central ingredients 29; in daily life 30–31; history of 23–27; practical considerations 20; *see also* centering prayer; Ignatian prayer; Jesus Prayer; "prayer of the senses"; welcoming prayer
control 24, 72–73, 75, 76, 92–93, 110
Corinthians 66, 76, 102, 103, 106–107, 124
cup metaphor 77, 88, 104, 124

daily examen 47–49, 51, 52
David 47–48
decision making 11, 13
deification 27–28
depression 17
detachment 24, 87, 94–95
distractions 20, 26, 31, 123; *apophatic* prayer 25; centering prayer 71, 78–79, 82, 97; freedom from 88, 94; "prayer of the senses" 40
divine providence: conformity to divine providence exercise 49–50, 52; surrender to 49–50, 52, 117–125; *see also* God, providence of
divorce 6, 51, 67
"doing" mode 101n1, 107–108, 110
Dugas, M. 8n2, 9, 11, 16

Eastern Orthodox Church 24, 55–56
Ecclesiastes 93
emotional distress 10; *see also* inner distress
emotions 47, 106

INDEX

empathy 55, 59, 60, 61, 66
Esther 117–118
exhaustion 1, 75–76
exposure therapy 106

faith 49, 78, 79, 80, 85, 91, 94
false self 70, 72–75, 76, 85
fear 106
feedback 11
Finley, James 31, 89–90, 122
forgiveness 57, 96
Foster, R. 18, 40, 87
freedom 24, 87–88, 94

Garden of Gethsemane 22, 89
generalized anxiety disorder (GAD)
    1, 5, 7, 16
Genesis 27, 57, 90, 119, 121
gentle approach to life 90–91
goals 7, 19
God: *apophatic* prayer 24–25, 78; attributes of 3; case
    examples 6, 7, 36–37, 51–52, 67–68, 85–86, 124;
    centering prayer 19, 70–72, 75–82, 85–86, 87–97; *The
    Cloud of Unknowing* 26; daily examen 47–49, 51; Ignatian
    prayer 39–40, 52–53; Jesus Prayer 19, 54, 56–61, 66–68;
    mercy of 66; "prayer of the senses" 40–44; presence of
    5, 48, 68, 70, 80, 81, 86, 88, 91, 102, 105; providence of
    16–20, 24, 29–30, 49–50, 52, 73–74, 87–88, 104–105,
    114, 117–124; receptivity 77–78; relationship with 1;
    Serenity Prayer 21; sitting in silence with 2, 4, 5, 17–18,
    22, 25, 36, 71, 75; *theosis* 27–28; time for prayer 30–32;
    welcoming prayer 19–20, 102–115
goodness 2, 3, 4, 17, 87, 94, 96
Gorman, M. 95
grace 31, 93, 105, 121; centering prayer 72, 76, 90; Jesus
    Prayer 57, 59; trust in God's 96; welcoming prayer
    102, 106, 107
Greek Orthodox Church 27, 55–56
Gregory the Great 2, 72

Haisten, C. 115n1, 115n2
healing 118
Hebrews 28
hesychia 55–56, 58, 59
homework: centering prayer 85, 100; introduction to
    contemplative practice 36; Jesus Prayer 66; "prayer of
    the senses" 50; welcoming prayer 114
hope 5, 21, 50
humility 25, 28
hupomone 5

Ignatian prayer 19, 39–53; *see also* "prayer of the senses"
Ignatius Loyola 39, 42, 47
imagination 39, 40, 89
Immanuel 108, 115
inner distress 40–41, 104, 105, 106–107, 114, 115
integrative model 16–17
intimacy 18, 29, 58, 60
intolerance of uncertainty (IU) 4–5, 9–10, 13, 16, 17, 25
Isaiah 108
"It Is Well with My Soul" (Spafford) 120

Jesuits 39, 52, 115n2
Jesus Christ 2, 3, 18, 21, 124; *apophatic* prayer 78; "being"
    with 107, 108, 110; "contemplative attitudes" 95–96;
in the Garden of Gethsemane 22, 89; gentle approach
    of 90–91; God's providence 15; *hupomone* 5; mercy
    of 54–55, 56–57, 59, 60, 65–66, 91; mindset of 87;
    name of 54, 55; parable of the vine and branches
    119; "prayer of the senses" 41, 42–43, 50, 51; rest
    92; self-emptying love 76–77; sitting in silence with
    75; spiritual presence of 108; surrender to God 88,
    89–90, 95, 118; teaching on worry 16–17; *theosis*
    27–28, 95; three-minute breathing with 30, 121–122;
    welcoming prayer 109–110, 114, 115
Jesus Prayer 19, 23, 24, 29, 53, 54–69; 20-minute
    exercise 60–61, 66; benefits of the 57–58; brief history
    of the 54–55; case examples 67–68; centering prayer
    76; Eastern Orthodox Church 55–56; homework 66;
    instructions for the 59; journaling 63–65, 66; main
    ingredients of the 56–57; recording your efforts 62;
    reflection exercise 57; *theosis* 27
John 54, 55, 89, 90–91, 95, 119, 121
journaling: centering prayer 83–85, 98–100;
    introduction to contemplative practice 33–35, 36;
    Jesus Prayer 63–65, 66; "prayer of the senses" 44–46,
    50; welcoming prayer 111–114
Julian of Norwich 24

kataphatic tradition 24, 25, 29, 78
Keating, T. 18, 72–73, 81, 88, 91, 92, 96
kenosis 76–77, 86, 95; *see also* self-emptying
Knabb, Joshua J. 8n1, 8n2
knowledge 2, 3, 4, 17, 103

Laird, M. 18
language 24, 25, 29
Lazarus 55
lectio divina 24, 40
"letting go" 30, 49; centering prayer 91; welcoming
    prayer 105, 109, 110
Lewis, C.S. 104
location for prayer 20
Lord's Prayer 95–96, 119
love 3, 29, 118; centering prayer 72, 80, 85; *The Cloud of
    Unknowing* 26; Jesus Prayer 61; self-emptying 76–77;
    trust in God's 2, 4, 17, 79, 102, 104
Luke 1, 80, 94; cup metaphor 77, 88, 104, 124; Garden
    of Gethsemane 22; Mary and Martha 20, 26, 102,
    103, 107–108, 115n2, 121; mercy 66

Mark 3
Martha 26, 102, 107–108, 110, 115n2
Mary 20, 26, 102, 103, 107–108, 109, 115n2, 121
Matthew 9, 52, 68, 94, 104, 124; earthly treasures 70, 72;
    Garden of Gethsemane 89; God's providence 15, 74;
    Immanuel 108; Jesus' calming of the storm 60; Jesus'
    teachings on worry 16–17, 18, 19, 41, 95; Lord's
    Prayer 95–96, 119; meditative bible reading 40; mercy
    54–55; rest 92; surrender to God's will 118
MBCT *see* mindfulness-based cognitive therapy
meditation 4, 30; centering prayer 81–82, 96–97;
    Ignatian prayer 39; Jesus Prayer 60–61; "prayer of the
    senses" 40, 41–43, 50; welcoming prayer 109–110
Meister Eckhart 24
mercy 31, 54–55, 91, 105, 121; centering prayer 72, 90; Jesus
    Prayer 53, 56–59, 60, 61, 65–66, 67; trust in God's 96
mindfulness 4
mindfulness-based cognitive therapy (MBCT) 8n1, 102,
    107, 108, 121

127

Mount of Olives 77
Mrozowski, Mary 115n1

Nassif, B. 27–28
New Testament 5, 55, 59
Niebuhr, Reinhold 21
non-judgment 4, 19–20, 31, 109
Nouwen, Henri 77, 87–88

obedience 28, 95
openness 89
Origen 55

pain 103–105, 106, 108, 114, 115; *see also* suffering
patience 5
Paul 28, 55, 66, 76, 77, 87, 95, 106–107
peace 49, 56, 92, 103–104, 115n2, 118
Pennington, B. 78, 79–80
Peter 27, 28
Philippians 28, 76, 77, 87, 95, 115, 123
Philokalia 24, 27, 55–56
power 3, 118; centering prayer 80, 85; false self 72–73; trust in God's 2, 4, 17, 79, 87, 94, 102, 104; in weakness 95
"prayer of the senses" 24, 25, 29, 39, 40–47; 20-minute exercise 41–43, 50; case examples 51, 52; homework 50; journaling 44–46, 50; recording your efforts 43
prayer word 26, 71, 76, 78, 81–82, 88, 91, 96–97
presence 3, 68; centering prayer 70, 71, 80, 81, 86; consenting to God 88, 91; daily examen 48; of Jesus 108–109; trust in God's 2, 4, 17; welcoming prayer 102, 105, 109–110
problem solving 11, 13, 119
procrastination 11
Psalms 3, 23, 47, 48, 55, 94, 105, 123

Rakestraw, R. 27
receptivity 77–78
relationships 6–7
renunciation 24
rest 75–76, 91–92, 104
"rest in God" 2, 72
Robichaud, M. 8n2, 9, 11, 16

safety 24, 70, 72, 73, 85, 87
Sayings of the Desert Fathers 23–24
security 24, 72, 73, 75, 76, 87
Segal, Z. 31, 101n1, 122
self: autonomous 94; false 70, 72–75, 76, 85; idea of 76
self-emptying 24, 70, 76–77, 86, 95
self-esteem 72, 73, 76
self-worth 72, 75
Serenity Prayer 21
silence 18, 24, 37, 75, 82, 96, 97
simple life 89–90, 96
Solomon, King 93
Spafford, Horatio 120
spirit 57
"spirit of poverty" 87–88
Spiritual Exercises 39, 40, 42, 47
St. Augustine 88
St. Claude de la Colombière 8n2, 49, 50, 52, 53n1, 103–104, 115n2

St. John of the Cross 24
St. Theophan the Recluse 59
St. Theresa of Avila 24
status 70
stillness 37, 55–56, 58, 59, 88
stress 17, 103
suffering 55, 104, 106, 108, 115n2; *see also* pain
surrender 31, 32, 37; *apophatic* prayer 25; benefits of 118–119; case examples 124; centering prayer 29, 70–71, 76–77, 80–82, 85–86, 88, 91–92, 96–97; distracting thoughts 79; to divine providence 49–50, 52, 117–125; Ignatian prayer 40; Jesus Prayer 58, 60, 65, 68; key Bible verses 123; as lifelong pursuit 119; "three-minute breathing with Jesus" 121–122; welcoming prayer 103, 104–105, 106, 107, 110, 114–115

Talbot, J. 57, 59, 66
theosis 24, 27–28, 95
Thessalonians 55, 58
"three-minute breathing with Jesus" 30, 121–122
time 30–31
Timothy 119
Trinity 56, 59
trust 4, 104, 118, 124; centering prayer 80, 86, 96; children 72; "spirit of poverty" 88; welcoming prayer 102, 103, 105, 115
Trustful Surrender to Divine Providence 49–50

uncertainty 1–2, 29; case examples 6–7, 36–37, 52, 86, 114–115, 124; centering prayer 70, 80, 83, 87, 89, 91; daily examen 48–49; distracting thoughts 78–79; "doing" mode 107; Ignatian prayer 40; intolerance of 4–5, 9–10, 13, 16, 17, 25; Jesus Prayer 53, 56, 57–58, 60–61, 65; just "being" 93–94; letting go of 30, 91; relationship with worry 9–22; responses to 11–12; self-emptying 77; surrender to God 124; welcoming prayer 102, 103, 105, 109, 115
"unloading" 92

value 70
vine and branches, parable of the 119

welcoming prayer 19–20, 24, 30, 102–116; 20-minute exercise 109–110, 114; case examples 114–115; homework 114; instructions for the 109; journaling 111–114; main ingredients of the 105; overview of the 103–105; presence of Jesus 108–109; recording your efforts 110–111
wisdom 3, 118; centering prayer 80, 86; trust in God's 2, 4, 17, 79, 87, 94, 96, 102, 104, 114
worry: case examples 6–7, 86, 114–115; centering prayer 70, 80, 83, 87, 89, 91; Christian view of 2–3, 19, 20; in contemporary Western society 1; daily examen 48–49; definition of 17; distracting thoughts 78–79; "doing" mode 107; Ignatian prayer 40; integrative model 16–17; Jesus Prayer 53, 54, 56, 58, 60–61, 66; just "being" 93–94; letting go of 30, 49, 91; positive beliefs about 15–16; "prayer of the senses" 42–43; psychological understanding of 2; self-emptying 77; surrender to God 124; uncertainty and 9–22; welcoming prayer 102, 103, 105, 109, 115
worry log 13–14
worst-case scenarios 13